# Advance praise for *Finding*

"With the intimacy of a sharing circle, this story draws in our hearts immediately. Pulsing between difficult observations and skilfully woven into *Finding Otipemisiwak* are Indigenous teachings and poetry, allowing the narrative to breathe. Even in the very wake of hardship, Andrea Currie encourages us to believe in the enduring powers of culture, earth, and community."
—SHALAN JOUDRY, author of *Waking Ground*

"*Finding Otipemisiwak* is a stunning, illuminating, and gutting journey through the life of a Sixties Scoop survivor. Page turning, genre bending, personal and political, staggeringly honest, heartbreaking and glorious, it is a story of resistance, possibility, healing, and hope, of reclamation and reconciliation. This book is part of the truth-telling change this country so desperately needs."
—CAMILLE FOUILLARD, author of *Precious Little*

"Weaving myriad forms—poetry, family history, personal essay, cultural criticism—Andrea Currie tells her story with mercy and force, revealing the warp and weft of the racist system that codified the robbery of Indigenous children through the Sixties Scoop and the devastating consequences. In this rigorous and beautiful debut, Currie's unfaltering pursuit of complicated truths lifts into the light the possibility of healing. *Finding Otipemisiwak* is a necessary, searing, and luminous gift of a book."
—REBECCA SILVER SLAYTER, author of *The Second History*

"*Finding Otipemisiwak* is a beautifully written story of tragedy and triumph, as well as one of escape from a false family into the embrace of a loving one. Threading through Andrea Currie's remarkable tale is a heart-wrenching bond between her and her adoptive brother, Rob. This book contains a story that desperately needs to be told."
—FRANK MACDONALD, author of *A Forest for Calum*

"*Finding Otipemisiwak* is a poignant story of self-discovery, weaving Red River Métis heritage with personal narrative and ancestral lore and honouring resilience amidst the Sixties Scoop."
—ALBERT G.D. BECK, director of the Manitoba Métis Federation

# FINDING OTIPEMISIWAK

# FINDING OTIPEMISIWAK

## The People Who Own Themselves

ARSENAL PULP PRESS
VANCOUVER

# Andrea Currie

ARSENAL PULP PRESS
Suite 202 – 211 East Georgia St.
Vancouver, BC V6A 1Z6
Canada
*arsenalpulp.com*

The publisher gratefully acknowledges the support of the Canada Council for the Arts and the British Columbia Arts Council for its publishing program and the Government of Canada and the Government of British Columbia (through the Book Publishing Tax Credit Program) for its publishing activities.

Arsenal Pulp Press acknowledges the xʷməθkʷəy̓əm (Musqueam), Sḵwx̱wú7mesh (Squamish), and səlilwətaɬ (Tsleil-Waututh) Nations, custodians of the traditional, ancestral, and unceded territories where our office is located. We pay respect to their histories, traditions, and continuous living cultures and commit to accountability, respectful relations, and friendship.

Quotations from "Blood Memory" are reprinted with permission of Nola Turner-Jensen.

Lyrics to "Livin' the Blues" are reprinted with permission of Gary Hines.

Lyrics to "Buried Truth" are reprinted with permission of DeeDee Austin.

Quotation from NECESSARY LOSSES by Judith Viorst copyright © 1986 Judith Viorst. Reprinted with the permission of Simon & Schuster. All rights reserved.

Cover and text design by Jazmin Welch
Cover art by Tracy Charette Fehr, *Northwest*, 2022, 10' × 13', stitched, beaded, and painted textile maps
Edited by Catharine Chen
Proofread by Alison Strobel

Printed and bound in Canada

Library and Archives Canada Cataloguing in Publication:
Title: Finding Otipemisiwak : the people who own themselves / Andrea Currie.
Names: Currie, Andrea (Andrea M.), author.
Identifiers: Canadiana (print) 20240334663 | Canadiana (ebook) 20240334698 | ISBN 9781551529554 (softcover) | ISBN 9781551529561 (EPUB)
Subjects: LCSH: Currie, Andrea (Andrea M.) | LCSH: Currie, Andrea (Andrea M.)—Family. | LCSH: Métis—Ethnic identity. | LCSH: Sixties Scoop, Canada, 1951–ca. 1980.
Classification: LCC FC113 .C87 2024 | DDC 305.897/071—dc23

*for Rob*

The process of remembering things from long ago,
and healing through them, is a pursuit of sovereignty.

—HELEN KNOTT

Still, a book, which coaxes confession,
seems too flimsy for all this longing.

—BILLY-RAY BELCOURT

## Author's Note

Some names and identifying details have been changed to protect the privacy of certain individuals.

Sometimes it's necessary to write about things that can be hard to read. This book contains brief accounts of physical and emotional child abuse. Take care of yourself, whatever that looks like for you. Love and resistance will also be found within.

# CONTENTS

## III

## Interlude

# INTRODUCTION

Dust motes dance in a slant of light falling on a dog-eared cardboard box being opened. Stacks of dusty journals that haven't seen daylight for years stare up at her. In one cloth-bound volume, these words: *Since nobody has written what I need to read, I'll have to write it myself.*

●●●

The Sixties Scoop has lurked in the shadows of our collective awareness for a long time. As survivors of Indian residential schools in this coun try we call Canada began to speak, chipping away at the wall of silence that the dominant culture has built and maintained over centuries of settler colonialism, some of them insisted that residential schools weren't the only genocidal attempt to wipe Indigenous Peoples off the face of our own homelands. They pointed out that the colonizers have perpetrated many assaults against us since their arrival, including the spreading of disease, the criminalization of our ceremonies, the double-speak distraction of making treaties with us while continuing to steal our lands, the passing of the racist Indian Act, the forced relocations, and the residential schools, which, as they became unpalatable to the Canadian people whose appetite for erasing us was still unsatiated, morphed into the use of the child welfare system to steal our children and destroy our kinship systems.

These emotionally and spiritually crippling blows to Indigenous individuals and communities reverberate to this day through the obscenely low level of funding and resources for Indigenous children and families in need of support, well documented and articulated by Cindy Blackstock, executive director of the First Nations Child & Family Caring Society of Canada (FNCFCS). In 2007, Blackstock filed a complaint with the Canadian Human Rights Tribunal (CHRT), claiming that the federal government had been negligent and discriminatory in its treatment of Indigenous children in care. The Tribunal ruled in favour of Blackstock and the FNCFCS and ordered the federal government to close the funding gap between Indigenous and non-Indigenous child welfare agencies and to compensate the children and families torn apart by these racist policies. However, the federal government blatantly refused to comply with these orders and appealed to the Federal Court of Canada. The Federal Court upheld the CHRT's ruling, and in response the federal government appealed that decision as well, using the time-(dis)honoured tactic of citing jurisdictional issues, causing further delays and more suffering for Indigenous children and families. Blackstock and the FNCFCS continued to fight for the children, youths, and families who were impacted by this injustice. In July of 2023, the CHRT issued a decision letter finding that the Final Settlement Agreement signed by the FNCFCS, the Assembly of First Nations, Canada, and other parties to the class action satisfies the Tribunal's compensation orders. Compensation will not go to the children and families right away, however. At the time of writing, a distribution protocol, which will outline who is eligible for compensation, is being drawn up and will need to be approved. Indigenous survivors of the child welfare system are still waiting to see justice.[1]

The colonial assault on our peoples continues.

The *Sixties Scoop* is the term used to refer to a period of time during the 1960s into the mid-1970s when provincial child welfare agencies removed children from Indigenous families and communities and placed them for adoption into white homes. The prevailing practice at that time was to deny adopted children any access to information about or contact with our birth families, robbing Indigenous people like me of our identity and culture, a profound loss that was dismissed as inconsequential. After all, we were being given the opportunity to become white; what could we possibly have to complain about?

In June of 2015 I heard the news that the premier of Manitoba, the province that is on the traditional territory of my people, the Red River Métis, had publicly apologized for the forced adoption and relocation of Indigenous children in the Sixties Scoop. The feelings that flooded me like the Red River breaching its banks were unexpected.

Along with the Mi'kmaw residential school survivors of We'koqma'q First Nation in Unama'ki (Cape Breton), whom I've had the honour of accompanying on their healing journey for the past twenty years, I am cynical about these public and performative statements of apology made by politicians who are just as likely to be thinking about how Indigenous Peoples are the fastest-growing demographic in this country (read: lots of voters) as they are to be having genuine, soul-searching moments of remorse. And yet, when we hear the words *I am sorry*, many of us are overcome with intense emotions that surprise us.

Having our suffering acknowledged can be a powerful experience. Especially after years of living in the shadowy half-light of colonial erasure.

For the first thirty-eight years of my life, I had no idea who I was. Taken from my Métis family and community at birth in 1960, I was placed for adoption with the Curries, a white suburban family in Winnipeg. The material privileges that came with that placement were no match for the acute insecurity I experienced for the following seventeen years, a period of my life that was, hands down, the most difficult I have lived through. However benevolent the intentions of the assimilationist policy–driven social workers who put me there may have been, it turns out that infants and children are not tabulae rasae, blank slates upon which parents can project the image of the children they want to have and mould the little human beings in their care into those people. We now know that adopted children sustain a deep psychic wound from the separation from our birth mothers and experience profound, usually unacknowledged grief and loss, which is made worse when we are placed in cultures other than our own.

When an Indigenous person receives their Spirit Name, the power of that ceremony comes from our ancestors, strengthening our connection to All Our Relations and guides in the Spirit World, who gave us that name before we were born. It is a name that teaches us about our unique spirit and the gifts, also known as medicine, that we will carry and offer in the world during our lifetime. It is the name by which we are known in the Spirit World we came from and to which we will someday return. Being adopted doesn't change that, but being removed from our culture makes it harder for us to find our way as the people we were born to be.

Throughout the years that I lived in that adoptive home, the white middle-class family life of home, school, church, piano lessons, and camping trips that looked benign to outsiders was, in truth, spiked with physical and emotional abuse. I grew up thinking that I was a "bad kid" or "problem child" when in fact, I just couldn't hold the shape of the mould, couldn't be the daughter my mother was trying to make me into. It was clear to me from a young age that she had designs on who I should be. Despite my best efforts to adhere to the plan, I somehow always ended up being myself. In that world, not only was that not a good thing, it was a punishable offence of which I was constantly guilty.

Add to that the total lack of anything that could serve as context or reference point to help me understand why I was going through this, and the result is a childhood laced with guilt, shame, confusion, and loneliness. With the help of wise Elders and skilled therapists encountered later in my life, I have worked through a lot of this. The loneliness is still with me.

As the Sixties Scoop surfaces in the public consciousness, I sense a space opening up for a long-overdue conversation. A conversation that could address a lot of questions.

Why does the question "Who am I?" for some of us freeze the blood in our veins?

What is the nature of the injuries caused by the stealth bombs of cultural loss?

How does a person navigate the jagged, rocky road to reconnection, if that is even a possibility?

What is cultural blindness, and why is this form of impaired vision a quietly ignored health problem of epidemic scale all around us?

What is Indigenous identity in the aftermath of apocalyptic colonial destruction?

What can still grow in this wasteland of ash and weathered bone?

What can be healed, and what is broken beyond repair?

And most importantly, where is Trickster hiding our joy?

My journey back to myself has meandered as much as the rivers of my homeland. Along the way, Creator has guided me to Elders who have taught me many things, including humility. I know there's no way I can answer all these questions. What follows is my contribution to the conversation.

In writing the book I needed to read during those decades of searching for some way to recognize myself, someplace I would be seen, my hope is that someone will read this and feel less alone.

# Prelude

# THE LAND I BELONG TO

I

13,000 years ago
my homeland was a lake left behind
glaciers melted and receded
filling the bowl of the land I come from
holding the promise of peoples to come
holding more water than
all the lakes in the world today combined
8,000 years ago
Hudson Bay's ice melted, making mud
Lake Agassiz drained quietly away into
the Arctic Ocean
(a climate event associated by scholars with
the biblical story of the Great Flood)

1,000 feet deep
this continental bathtub emptied into
the great Mississippi and
knowing no borders
flowed all the way down into the
Gulf of Mexico

I was born on land that once was water
daughter in constant search for a shore
I played and swam in the relic of the *lak vyeu*
the ancient lake
known now as Lake Winnipeg
grown now
I live in a place
where dusk is defined
by an amphibious sun slipping down
behind a distant watery line

II

Agassiz left in its wake
three remnant lakes
nestled in a vast plain
endless fields of windblown grasses
groves of birch, poplar, alder
*paskwâwaskî*
threaded by rivers
veins of the land and
great marshy lungs
*maskîkwa*
refreshing prairie air

this fertile land
once a lake bottom
a great river's womb
gave birth to me

III

my Saulteaux grandmothers paddled these rivers
moved with the wind
*ohtin*
across the plains
sharing space with wild creatures
honouring the sacred
harvesting in harmony with the
land's rhythms of abundance
my grandfathers from France
given new boots and a long boat ride
sucked in the sea air and were
sucked in by lies about land for the taking
rash decisions and brash dreams of the
lives they would be making
upon arrival scorned life in colonial towns
scanned the western horizon for
other possible futures
finding a way through winding rivers, they
wound up on the prairies
foundlings at the mercy of the wary natives
and discovered something familiar
*taapishkooch*
a wildness in one another's eyes, an
inkling from which they fashioned kinship
they wed
one another and the limitless space
where the ghost of a memory of a lake
still blows across the land

Neither European or First Nation, the Métis were referred to by the Cree as *O-tee-paym-soo-wuk*, the people who own themselves.

—KELLY SAUNDERS, "No Other Weapon: Métis Political Organization and Governance in Canada"

I

fluorescent tubes
implanted in the ceiling
machines softly whirring
the neonatal ward
stark even at night
a world of half-light

swaddled in flannelette
washed too often to be soft
behind the transparent wall of clear plastic
a three-day-old baby
waits

basic needs met by
professional competence
mostly kind
many hands
mostly gentle
her first lesson learned
through her skin
only touched when
necessary

the mother does not come often
because after all
that would just make it harder
when she leaves for the last

time

stands still in that moment

a primal wound opens
that will never

completely

close

close

as in proximity

close

as in completion

beginnings and endings
fused
in faint patterns she traces
with tiny flailing fingers
as if finding a route to travel
on an invisible map

# ROB'S FIRST ARRIVAL

Whenever I am asked about my earliest memory, I see myself standing beside my adoptive mother, Irene, in front of the picture window in our house on Oakdean Boulevard, looking out. My older brother was standing there with us, neither of us old enough to be in school yet. I was glued to my spot, watching with intense anticipation—that feeling still so vivid—for the 1960s station wagon, a big boat of a car with wood panelling on the sides, driven by the social worker who was bringing my little brother, Rob, to live with us.

It was the spring of 1964. I was three years old, and Rob was two. I was the second child our parents adopted, he was the third and last. I adored him. We had already met, of course, on previous visits. But this was the Big Day: the little boy we called Robbie back then was coming to stay!

Robbie's favourite toy to play with when he came for visits was a rocking horse made by our adoptive dad. As soon as I saw the station wagon pull into our driveway, I turned and ran down to the family room in the basement. Standing two feet off the ground, with rockers about two-and-a-half feet long, the solid wooden rocking horse was almost as big as I was and definitely heavier. Still, with determination and strength fuelled by adrenalin, like a mother whose child is pinned under a car, I hauled and pulled and bumped the rocking horse up the stairs, bringing it to the living room so it would be there when Robbie walked in the front door. I got about halfway up the flight of stairs before I just couldn't go any farther. I didn't have the strength to get it all the way up to the main floor, and I knew I couldn't let it go. I was stuck. I hollered to my mom to come and help me. She did. Overruling my plan and my protests, she took the rocking horse back downstairs and left it there, and we returned to the living room to welcome Rob.

There is something about that moment that distills the forty-eight years of my relationship with Rob, before he crossed over to spirit at the age of fifty. That scene has a holographic quality, every element, every dimension of our relationship contained within it: the way his vulnerability reached into the deepest places in me, the way we understood each other, the unbreakable bond that sustained us through years of abuse and made us lifelong allies, the way I reached beyond reason to do whatever I could for him, my powerlessness.

We were two Métis Sixties Scoop adoptees. Our older brother, also adopted, was of European descent. For reasons I don't even want to get my head around, there was a disparity in our childhoods. Our older brother's was not punctuated by abuse; it was Robbie and I who were not pleasing to our parents. We were still quite young, though I don't recall exactly how old, when we acknowledged this shared experience. It was like that song on *Sesame Street* about how one of these things is not like the others, except with us, there were two that didn't belong. Try as we might—and we both did, we tried hard—we didn't fit in. I remember feeling anguish before I knew what it was, the feeling of not being the daughter my mother wanted, at a loss as to what I could do about it. And Rob—well, it was years later, in therapy, when I realized that my witnessing our mother's emotional and psychological cruelty toward him, as well as both parents' physically assaulting him, is the source of severe trauma I am still trying to heal from. My deepest grief wears his name.

Recently, I heard Jenny Heijun Wills read an excerpt from her award-winning memoir, *Older Sister. Not Necessarily Related.*, in which she shares the story of her reunion with the South Korean family she lost touch with when she was transnationally adopted. Wills teaches American literature and writing at the University of Winnipeg. She also teaches critical race studies, so her thinking on the topic of adoption, including her own, is informed by the recognition that racism is pervasive in society, embedded in and perpetuated by every institution. In the interview after her reading, Wills spoke about the dominant narratives of adoption and how they don't reflect the range of experiences of adoptees. Narratives like: it didn't matter to our parents who we, the adoptees, were or where we came from, because they just wanted to help. Or this one: adoption is blessing for those of us lucky enough to be chosen. Wills talked about how it actually isn't like that for a lot of adoptees. How some of us felt like props in the lives that our white middle-class adoptive parents were determined to construct.

Hearing that was like being hit by a Mack truck.

Rob and I were the props that didn't behave properly.

My adoptive mother has a wall-mounted black grosgrain ribbon with six small, circular brass frames attached to it. From top to bottom, the photos are: my older brother, then me, both of us about a year old, and then Robbie when he arrived, aged two and a half. So there are baby pictures of two of us, but Robbie was already a toddler by the time he arrived. His photo tells a heart-wrenching story. A sweet little boy with a pasted-on smile and a definite "deer in the headlights" look in his eyes. He had already been in several foster homes by then, considered "unadoptable" because of his asthma, eczema, and pigeon-toed feet. In hindsight, his being Métis might have had something to do with it too. My uncle Derry told me when I was a young adult, years after my parents had returned Rob to the Children's Aid Society at the age of fifteen, that for months after Rob arrived in our family, whenever we went anywhere, he would grab a fistful of our mother's skirt and refuse to let go. He was terrified to be left behind, an experience he had already been through several times before he came to us. Those emotional wounds were not mentioned among his "special needs."

Here comes the guilt: how can I write about our adoptions this way when our parents were basically good people who wanted to have children but were unable to conceive? People who *were* loving, in some ways? What about the good things we did together as a family? Don't those count for something?

And here's where I make the shift from feeling guilty—which I believe is a useless emotion, a contraction that makes a person feel small, not helpful at all in making change—to asking myself: What is my responsibility here?

My answer: I am responsible for being fair to our adoptive parents in my portrayal of them. But what is fair? In this instance, I take it to mean that I contextualize their attitudes and behaviour in the values of the settler colonial culture that shaped them. It means that I acknowledge their humanity and the possibility of past trauma in their lives that might help explain—though not excuse—their violence. It means that I consider how the beliefs about parenting that they inherited and that were reinforced by their social and religious communities influenced the choices they made as parents.

All children need safety, affirmation of their basic goodness, and unconditional love. All children need to be seen and appreciated for their uniqueness. My parents' inability to provide this emotional sustenance to Rob and me is partly on them and partly on the parenting practices of their generation, which favoured corporal punishment and unquestioning respect for authority, condoning both harsh rigidity and physical violence. Their seeming total ignorance when it came to Rob's need for even *more* tenderness and affirmation as a result of the damage done to him through repeated experiences of abandonment (something that was obvious to me from early on)—that's on the child welfare system. Rob and I needed to be with our own people, where we would have grown up held steady in the kinship of our Métis community, the community's arms embracing troubled families like ours, letting us know that we belonged and were safe inside an experience of family that was bigger than the terrifying, insular radius of one emotionally impaired woman who felt compelled to be a mom.

Jeannine Carrière, scholar and professor in the School of Social Work at the University of Victoria, states in her study on the importance of cultural planning when Indigenous children are being adopted that connection to one's family and community is needed for healthy identity development in general, as well as for racial identity development. Raven Sinclair, a scholar and social work professor at the University of Regina, recommends that when a non-Indigenous family adopts an Indigenous child, the entire family should shift its identity to become bicultural, seeking relationships with the Indigenous community their adopted child comes from and learning teachings from that nation that will enrich *all* members of the adoptive family.[2] Carrière states that cultural plans in the adoptions of Indigenous children "help to end the mass emotional and psychological trauma children are experiencing when they are not connected to their culture."[3]

This much-needed development in responding to the needs of Indigenous adoptees did not come soon enough for Rob and me. Our parents expected us to assimilate easily into their world, and when we did not, the problems that ensued were not interpreted with any socio-cultural awareness but were seen by them to be due to personal deficiencies in us that it was their job to correct, usually with harsh discipline. The fact that this was not entirely their fault does not change the harm that was done to us at their hands.

Over and over again, Rob absorbed the blows of abandonment, all layered on top of the profound disorientation of cultural dislocation and loss. He needed to be with people who understood the impact that making and breaking bonds with numerous caregivers had on a baby's and a toddler's heart, mind, spirit, and body. Who understood the depth and breadth of the impact when a child experiences this repeatedly in the first three years of their life. Those who were responsible for Rob's care should have made sure my parents understood this and screened them for their capacity to love this child abundantly and consistently enough to help him heal. But they didn't.

Emotional and physical violence, even if its source is trauma in the perpetrator's life, is the responsibility of the human being who commits it. No matter how we're raised, it's our responsibility as adults to know what violates another person and to draw lines that we won't cross. If our empathy is muted or absent in moments of frustration and stress, we have healing to do ourselves. Our parents were products of an era in which the long-term impact of violence on children was not as well understood as it is now. Whatever their own experiences, our parents had not done their own healing. As adults raising children of their own, they were neither innocent nor monolithic villains.

There was malice in our home though. Rob and I grew up with that sharp blade held against our hearts, under the ice-cold gaze of our mother's pale-blue eyes.

I wonder now how much I understood that this would be the case, back then on that day of Rob's arrival, my earliest memory. At three, had I already been hit and hurt by our adoptive parents? Was I already scared of them? Probably. I remember witnessing our parents being extremely violent with Rob during his preschool years. How much of my own experience was woven into my overwhelming need to help him feel safe and know that he belonged, know that someone had really *seen* him, enough to want his favourite toy to be the first thing he saw when he walked through our door on the day he came to stay?

We heard the sound of two car doors closing, one after the other, and then the doorbell rang. The social worker came in, Robbie's small hand clasped tightly in hers. He was wearing shorts with a little polo shirt tucked in at the waistband and special shoes that didn't look very comfortable. There was a baffled look on his face, a sweetness I would come to cherish, and just the hint of a tentative smile.

"No, Mom, No!
I'm sorry, Mom, I'm sorry! PLEASE, MOM, DON'T!"
Terror and urgency in the little boy's voice.
Pleading, choking out words between sobs.
He is not yet in school.
He is still so small that he has to stand on a kitchen chair.
Otherwise, she would not be able to hold his tiny hand over the red-hot element.
His hand held in the vise grip of hers, her voice like steel.
"You've been told many times."
Sobs turn into screams.
I have gravitated to the doorway of the kitchen and stand in the hall, still and quiet as a statue.
I always have to be close to him when they are hurting him.
I don't know why—my presence makes no difference.
I am only one year older. There is nothing I can do to protect him.
She says: "You have to learn not to play with matches."
We say: nothing.
Our voices silenced in a deep-freeze of powerlessness.

# NIIZHOZIIBEAN—TWO RIVERS I

The Assiniboine River wound through my life before it and my story both merged with the Red River at Niizhoziibean, Anishinaabemowin for "two rivers," known in English as the Forks. Now the centre of the city of Winnipeg, Niizhoziibean is where the rivers become one and where I become whole, reuniting with the people I come from, turning, returning.

The Assiniboine rises in the southeast of what is now the province of Saskatchewan, fed by the Lilian and Whitesand rivers, swelling into the Lake of the Prairies. Flowing eastward from the lake, the river cuts through a break in an ancient geological formation known as the Manitoba Escarpment, between Riding Mountain and Turtle Mountain, and is joined in Manitoba by the Qu'Appelle and Souris rivers.

It gets its name from a group of Plains Indigenous people who had broken with the larger Sioux Nation in the early 1600s and formed a military and trade alliance with the Woodland Cree. Although the Assiniboine referred to themselves as Nakota, the Anishinaabeg introduced them to the French fur traders as *asinii bwaan*, which translated into English as the Stone Sioux, because they are the people "who cook by placing hot stones in water." This was shortened to Stonies, which was what the traders from both the Hudson's Bay and North West companies called them.

The Red River originates farther south, at the confluence of the Bois de Sioux and Otter Tail rivers, beginning its northward journey as a border between what are now the states of Minnesota and North Dakota. It spans over 600 of its 880 kilometres before crossing what is now a border into Manitoba and flowing farther north on a gradual downward slope for another 175 kilometres before pouring itself into Lake Winnipeg.

As far back as six thousand years ago, my Saulteaux ancestors paddled these waterways, fishing for walleye, pike, and bass, harvesting mussels and duck eggs, trapping *amikwag* and *wazhashkwag*, beaver and muskrat. Salamanders and turtles observed them from the banks, shaded by willow boughs. Kingfishers chattered overhead. The Saulteaux hauled their canoes up on the riverbank at the Forks, cut saplings and birchbark and made wigwams, dried fish, held council and ceremony, and traded with their neighbours, the Plains Cree, for whom the spot was also a traditional gathering place. At day's end, their eyes followed the sun's path toward the western horizon, watching the fiery orb drop below the treeline across the river now known as the Assiniboine.

Wednesday mornings before dawn, no matter the weather, my brothers and I were up at 5 a.m., folding flyers. We bundled up in our parkas, toques, and mittens, slung canvas bags stuffed with flyers crosswise over our shoulders, and headed out into the dark, frigid morning. Our warm breath made tiny, prickly ice in the woollen fibres of the scarves wrapped around our small faces. We each delivered to every house on two streets and the avenues in between, together covering the entire neighbourhood known as Woodhaven. My share of the route included Assiniboine Avenue, which meant tramping down the long driveways to houses nestled in deep wooded riverfront lots. There was a mystery to these homes; they seemed to me then to occupy another world, set apart from the rest of the neighbourhood. Because I knew—even though I couldn't see it from the front steps, where I placed flyers in mailboxes as quietly as I could so as not to disturb the sleeping occupants inside— that on the other side of these houses was the Assiniboine River.

I knew it was there, magnetically appealing whether seen or unseen, always moving, night and day. I envied the people lucky enough to have the river in their backyard. I felt drawn to its energy without knowing why. Its presence just a block and a half away from my own house was an unexplainable comfort.

I kicked at the loose pieces of asphalt where the street was crumbling around the edges. The Winnipeg summer sun beat down, even though it was still early. I loved feeling its heat caught in my almost-black hair, finding excuses to smooth down my pixie cut so I could feel that heat on my hands. The four of us were standing at the side of the street on Oakdean Boulevard, not far from the driveway of Cathy Blackwood's house, and I didn't know what to say.

Cathy was British because her grandparents came from England, Hanna Svensen's grandparents were born in Sweden, and Johanna Fischer's came from Germany.

"What are *you*, Andrea?" Cathy had asked.

I felt like I'd just been grabbed in a game of freeze tag, paralyzed, a nameless fear coursing through me. Lacking the concepts and language to parse the meaning of this question—it had to mean something, since we had stopped our game of hide-and-seek to answer it—I only knew two things: that I didn't know where I came from, and that admitting this was clearly not the right answer.

This is my earliest memory of understanding that I was different— that there was something everyone else knew about themselves, and they took that knowing for granted. I did not have this knowledge about myself. The importance of it was implied in Cathy's innocently demanding tone of voice; it hadn't occurred to her that this could be a difficult question for some eight-year-olds to answer.

My thumping heartbeat told me this was an interrogation, that I was an imposter, and my cover was about to be blown. I probably said something about being Belgian and British, since my mother's parents had emigrated from Belgium to Canada when they were teenagers, and I knew that some of my dad's people came from England. But I knew it wasn't true that I was Belgian and British, and it always felt weirdly shameful to say that as if it were true. I was adopted, that much I had always known. That fact was flat and final—no texture of story, of culture, no shadowy faces of ancestors. Matter-of-factly blank.

As blank as the rest of the conversation, which has not stayed with me. I don't remember exactly how I responded to Cathy's genealogical inquest.

What I remember is that pause.

What it feels like to have to pause when someone asks you who you are, who your people are, where you come from.

What it feels like to have your mask ripped off unexpectedly in the middle of playing with your friends, a mask you have worn since before you could think, now almost skin.

# LIVING THE NIGHTMARE II

I couldn't remember anything about my childhood before the age of twelve. The psychiatrist had me stand at one end of the big front room of his Victorian home in the south end of Halifax, imagine a line on the floor that spanned my life thus far, and walk backward slowly on this line as if backing up into my past. He walked beside me, facing me, watching me closely. I don't know what he saw, but suddenly he gently pulled me to the side so that I stepped off the imaginary line.

"What are you thinking about right now?"

I had gone back to a day I hadn't thought about for years.

*Something is going to happen.*
*Tension sizzles in the air.*
*Little hairs on my arm are sticking straight up, nerves are frying.*
*Dad is taking Robbie downstairs to the bedroom he built for my two brothers.*
*I follow, unnoticed.*
*Robbie starts to whimper.*
*As always, I get as close as I can—the next room, the family room.*
*I get down on my knees, tears already streaming down my face.*
*I don't know what Dad is doing to him.*
*Robbie's screams are the worst I've ever heard.*
*Worse than the time Mom held his hand so, so close to the hot element on the stove.*
*The screams pierce my bones and chill the blood in my veins.*

I hear them still, in moments of despair, wondering if I will ever heal from this. Knowing Rob did not. I found out afterward that Dad had burned my brother's thumbnail with a match. Again, in order to teach him not to play with matches.

In that session with the psychiatrist, I learned that witnessing abuse is also actually abuse. I told the psychiatrist the story, repeating my parents' justifications for what I can now see was torture: they had to get him to stop playing with matches, and they had tried everything.

When the psychiatrist asked, "Why didn't they just lock up the matches?" I looked at him as if he were speaking another language.

Driving home that day, I could feel the architecture of my psyche renovating itself, as if walls were moving around, the foundation and very structure of my being changing. It's lucky I didn't drive off the Macdonald Bridge on my way home to my downtown Dartmouth apartment. My attention was riveted inward.

Terrorizing Robbie to "teach" him?

What does terror truly teach but who to fear, who is unsafe?

What does a small child do when their parents are the ones to fear, and nowhere is safe?

Every second week for a full year, my skilful therapist dislodged the barbaric belief system I had internalized as a child, and questions I had never thought to ask surfaced. What other beliefs formed in my childhood were grotesquely wrong? How many of them was I still carrying?

# NIIZHOZIIBEAN—TWO RIVERS II

The Assiniboine River's current is fast and strong in the spring, the water frigid. Fed by copious amounts of snow from our infamous Manitoba winters, it gathers speed and greets the change of season with high energy. Waterfowl returning from their time down south can be heard along the river, quacking and honking as they select spots to build their nests along its banks. Songbirds come out in full chorus, with lots to say after their winter travels, alighting on the sunlit branches of the overhanging maple and willow trees, perched in the golden green glow of the infant leaves. Some trees grow so close to the river's edge that their trunks are partly in the water.

Spring is also the time when whole groves of tall trees appear to be growing in the river, caught in a meander with the overflow on all sides. Because part of the river's nature, well known to all who live along its banks, is to flood. It's hard to control a river. It will flood, even if those breaching waters wreak havoc in the homes and lives of people who live a stationary lifestyle, dotted all along the riverbanks. Even if it forces them to move, temporarily, at least. It's nothing personal. It's just the river's nature, the fascinating dance that ensues when water and land have a close relationship.

In my mind's eye, I see my ancestors shaking their heads as they watched the settlers hard at it, building their homesteads along the river. They would have thought: *waabishkiiweg ningiiwanaadiz!* Those white people are crazy!

I grew up on a flood plain. But that was only one of the ways the river marked the arrival of spring.

The host of the morning radio show had just broadcast the news and weather. Spring in Winnipeg arrived decisively. From one day to the next, the sunshine was stronger, the birds were back and singing away, and melting snow on sidewalks formed little rivulets we floated twigs on, sloshing through the puddles to follow them on their travels until they snagged on a drain cover. Each spring, we waited for the day the morning show host would announce, "We have reports that the ice on the river is breaking up ..."

The ice floes!

We bundled up, because even on warm and sunny spring days, the air was chilled by the lingering snow and ice, and joined the throng of Winnipeggers lining the stone walls of the Assiniboine Park Footbridge to look at—and listen to—the booming, cracking, bobbing chunks of ice bumping into and repelling each other as the spring current jostled them downstream. It was hard to get a spot where you could watch the ice floes crash their way through the bridge supports; the sides of the bridge were crowded, three or four people deep. But if you were patient, you'd get your turn. Parents and older siblings heard the cries of the little ones—"Let me see! I wanna see!"—and hoisted the small people up to get a look. Some watched from the bank on the Portage Avenue side of the river, where a clearing offered an easy way to get to the river's edge. But the bridge was the place to be. I remembered the collective catching of breath that time a dog became stranded on one of the ice floes and the in-unison sigh of relief when that unwitting passenger of the ice raft made it back to shore.

Starting from the day we'd watch from the bridge as the ice floes made their noisy, dramatic way downstream, dreams of summer flew unfettered.

# LEAVING MY BODY

We left Woodhaven at the end of June one year and moved across Portage Avenue, a couple of kilometres east. Silver Heights was another white suburban neighbourhood. My brothers and I left behind the smallest elementary school in Winnipeg, which had fewer than two hundred students, and enrolled in the largest: five classes for each of grades one through six, twelve hundred students in all. It was a shock, to say the least.

No longer able to shout through the open upstairs-bedroom window to our friends next door, who would call back to us from their bedroom window to make plans to go outside and play. No longer able to stand at the end of our driveway and count at least six houses within view where other kids in my class lived.

It was a whole new world. Daunting, even for an outgoing child like me. It wasn't the friendliest neighbourhood. In the seven years that I lived on Strathmillan Road, I can't recall even one conversation with the neighbours who lived right next door. We eventually became friends with two families who lived within sight of our house but never met any of the others.

I've never been able to fathom the cruelty of children. Is it a kink in our wiring, an aberration of human nature? Or a remnant from an earlier point on our evolutionary path that compels us to identify the most vulnerable among us and attack them, as a group? I can think of one time in grade three when, seeking acceptance by my popular peers, I participated in picking on a girl whom others in our class picked on. I got caught and punished for it, as if the universe were sending me a clear message: this is not who you are. I was ordinarily the one who reached out to include the marginalized, once organizing a surprise party at my house—not a birthday, but just a party for the little girl in our class who was Jehovah's Witness and was never allowed to come to our birthday parties. I remember collecting a dime from each of the girls in our class and going to the local drugstore to buy her a Little Lady hair accessory gift set so she would have a present to open at her party.

I had an affinity for the underdog that I now know is one of the characteristics of my people. Throughout history, the Red River Métis have made relationships and created kinship with peoples who were feared, despised, and believed to be subhuman. This was about a shared way of life—we were all peoples of the land—and solidarity: we were all despised and put down by the European colonizers, so joining forces and working together to help each other just made sense. We stood stronger together to resist hostile takeovers of our territory, sharing a healthy skepticism and distrust of any foreign paternalistic power promising a better life that would displace the one we were quite content with. My blood memory of all of this asserted itself in small ways. Ways like organizing that classmate's party, when I did not accept a situation that felt unfair and did not hesitate to challenge the rules her parents imposed.

The version of a social conscience I grew up with was firmly rooted in the message we heard in our middle-class Catholic church: the poor will always be with us. We should help alleviate the suffering of "the poor." But working to change the structures that perpetuate economic inequity? Not so much. For me, challenging the status quo has always come naturally. I was more inclined to try to figure out what action I could take for someone who wasn't doing well than to pray for them. Making relationships to create strength where there is vulnerability and to combat isolation is literally in my blood. As my Métis Elders say: we wrote our treaties in DNA, understanding kinship as a source of security and a way to live in peace.

None of this did me any good at Strathmillan School. I was the underdog, and I was very much alone among my classmates, who were all of European descent.

I don't recall much about my first day of grade five, except that I was awed by the enormity of the school. It was across the street from our new house and took up a whole city block, its three wings connected by a hallway through the middle, like an *H* with an extra vertical line. I had never seen so many kids in one place in all my life. It took me a while to find my class, since there was a whole hallway of grade five classrooms. I loved school, though, and was eager to make new friends. Unfortunately, the kids in my class were not as eager to befriend me.

Whether my adoptive mother set me up to stand out the way I did or whether she was oblivious to the brutal impact her strict rules had on my life, I can't say for sure. In any case, I wore cat-eye glasses that had most definitely gone out of style in favour of the wire frames worn by everyone else who had glasses, but my mother refused to get me a pair of those until I needed my prescription changed. My begging and pleading fell on deaf ears. On top of that, I had an uneven haircut she'd given me at home, with bangs that looked like they were cut with garden shears, and I was not allowed to wear jeans to school, although every single kid in my class wore jeans every day. In my godawful polyester pantsuits, with jagged hair and giant glasses, I was an easy target. The kindest words that one girl in my class who condescended to talk to me could offer were a suggestion that I sneak my jeans out of the house in the morning in a paper bag and change into them at school. There was no point telling her I didn't own any. I lived on that crumb of kindness for days.

Eventually, the daily bullying got the better of me, and one day I cried all the way home. When I walked into the house, my mother asked me what was wrong.

"N-nobody likes me here, Mom. I wa-want to go back to Woodhaven," I stuttered between sobs.

No hug, no words of reassurance. Just this cold reply, freeze-drying the tears on my face: "Well, remember, dear, you didn't have very many friends there either."

First of all, it was a lie. My Woodhaven memories are a blur of playing outside with friends, riding bikes, exploring the river and Sturgeon Creek, and skating on the rink my dad made by flooding our backyard with the hose every winter—it drew all the neighbourhood kids like a magnet. I'd always been with my friends. Second, what kind of mother says that to a tearful, heartbroken little girl having a hard time adjusting to a new school?

But I did not debate these points. I couldn't. I was no longer there. Whenever I recall this experience, it's as though I am watching through the chain-link fence in the playground directly across the street from our house, looking over at our blue bungalow, whose innocent-looking walls concealed such acts of cruelty. I know now that I left my body at that moment. I realized it years later, while working as a therapist and listening to one of my clients tell me about being severely beaten by their father and how, when this particular memory came to their mind, they saw themselves halfway up the stairs, looking down at themselves being beaten in the hallway below. This is the psyche's way of protecting us from the unbearable. In the range of responses to trauma that we now know as fight, flight, freeze, or fawn,[4] it is door number three. When we can't fight back, are not able to physically get away, and there is no way to "make nice," we "check out," going through the motions with our bodies while our brains do this neat trick of dissociation to remove us from the danger. Our spirit leaves our body, the only getaway possible under the circumstances.

That day is etched in my memory, a pivotal moment in my life. That was when I realized I could never go to my mother for comfort. I knew at the age of ten that I would never be safe with her. I turned away from that loss and went inward, finding solitary peace in an inner sanctum that has been my safe place ever since.

# Interlude

# LIGHT SHADOW BROTHER

there is a picture of you
you're looking down
at the tiny baby squirrel that you found

you had put it in the pocket of your T-shirt
it was scared
maybe as much as you
alone
as you were alone then too

your face is half in shadow
half in sunshine
a thin shaft of light
but it is there, all right

# II

When I was a little girl, clothes shopping with my mother was heart-wrenching.

I woke up on those mornings with dread and an anticipatory disappointment too big for my small years seeping into every thought, wearying me to the bone. I knew I would be forced to agree to wear things I hated, things that would either make me feel invisible or make me stand out in a bad way, things that would make me vulnerable. That was the point behind the saccharine wheedling and needling in my mother's voice. That was the sharp, jagged point.

When I was growing up, Winnipeg had a thriving garment industry that was just beginning to buckle under pressure from the cheaper labour and production costs elsewhere in the world. There were still dozens of garment factories, and my adoptive mother, bless her heart, knew where all the outlet stores were. She schooled me early on in the skills of bargain hunting—or "thrifting," as my adult son now calls it—skills that have served me well. She chose where we would shop. We never went to the HASH Jeans outlet, for instance, even though they were the coolest jeans in the seventies and were made locally. We went to stores that sold clothes she would wear.

I was quiet in the car while we drove to those places, into the older manufacturing and warehouse districts of the city, in the West End. From the dingy old buildings to the broken-down pavement in the parking lots to the scant customers in the stores, the atmosphere reinforced my sense that shopping was a joyless, utilitarian thing we did because clothes were a necessity.

In those stores, no effort was put into merchandising. The stock was dishevelled, with clumps of sweatpants next to a few hangers of silky shirts, winter jackets taking up the rest of the rack. Everything looked like it was made for older people. I learned to work fast to find one item that I liked. A plain sweater or simple skirt in a solid colour. Something I could make a pitch for that would make it easier to say no to the gaudy floral blouse or polyester pants my mother was sure to ask me to try on. She made endless efforts to persuade me of the merits of clothing I hated, her voice weirdly high pitched like she had just inhaled helium. The changing rooms were another battlefield. Sometimes I would actually try something on, and sometimes I would only pretend to, lying that whatever it was didn't fit. Sometimes she would make me try it on "again" so she could make up her own mind. I would politely refuse as many of her suggestions as I could, but her bizarre expectation that I should agree to let her dress me in her own image more often than not devolved into barked complaints and rigid insistence, which shut me down, defeated. Feeling as alone in the store with her as I was when facing the bullies at school, I would check out and go through the motions. The whole exercise was just another vehicle for her constant message that I could never be anything but the daughter whose existence she allowed.

I was worse than invisible. I wasn't actually there at all.

As a seedling barely out of the ground, I'd been ripped out by the roots and shoved into thin, acidic soil, where I grew into a paler version of myself, a shadowed outline. I was only ever a rough sketch that the woman who was legally my mother could rub out again and again, trying to make me come out right, until my skin tore like paper.

This is not just a metaphor. My skin literally tore, erupting in eczema so severe I had to stay home from school because wearing clothes was too painful. My mother took me to the family doctor and asked him, "What do you say, Jim? Should we trade her in?" He replied, "I don't know. She's got nice eyes." This family doctor didn't think to ask me if I was stressed about anything, unlike all the other health care providers who have since helped me learn how to heal and care for my skin. I could never tell him about the abuse. We sat in the pew across from his family in church, and his wife and my mother played bridge together on Wednesday nights.

Back then, I couldn't hope to be like all the fierce and self-possessed Métis women who came before me and were beautiful on their own terms; I didn't get to meet the ones who were still alive until my late thirties. Nor did I exist as the white middle-class daughter my mother wanted.

Bonsai is the Japanese art of miniaturization, pruning and shaping a tree so it appears to be mature but is so small it can live in a container. I was my mother's human bonsai project. I felt pressured by her to be smaller, less than, different from who I would be if I could grow naturally. Maybe she had been treated this way too when she was young. I don't know. All I know is that I was incessantly whittled and belittled, one twisted-up woman berating, negating, creating another. Pain ricocheted between us, boomerangs of broken dreams.

I can't recall exactly when I saw myself for the first time. Only that it was after I had left home, with only four items of clothing: a knee-length skirt I had made out of an old pair of jeans bought with my own money from my first part-time job; a dress I had bought myself at Clifford's, a dress shop downtown, for the time I asked my best friend out on a dinner date; a pair of olive-green cords; and an off-white Indian cotton shirt that went with the jean skirt and the cords.

The clothes shopping was just one microaggression in a childhood so replete with them that they blurred into a daily diet of just plain old aggression, constant and banal. When I left at seventeen, it wasn't because of the clothing, although that aspect did enable me to travel light.

I put everything I wanted to take with me into an old brown hard-sided suitcase handed down to me from my grandmother. There was a lot of empty space.

# LIVING THE NIGHTMARE III

*I am in my bedroom. The door is open.*
*Mom is there.*
*She is out of control.*
*She has a fistful of my hair in her left hand.*
*She is pulling me downward by my hair.*
*My scalp feels like it is being torn off, my back curving sharply in my attempt to lessen the pain.*
*I am trying to stay on my feet.*
*She pounds on my rounded back with her right hand closed into a fist.*
*She is kicking my legs.*
*I am yelling and crying.*
*She is yelling too, but I have no memory of what she is saying.*
*I have no memory of what I did to bring this on.*
*I have no memory of it ending or of what happened after.*
*I see this memory from the other side of my bedroom.*
*At some point, I must have checked out completely, because there is no context to this memory.*
*No before or after.*
*Just the terrifying image of a raging adult woman beating up a little girl.*

Maybe this is why TikTok doesn't appeal to me. I already have videos in my head on repeat.

# NIIZHOZIIBEAN–TWO RIVERS III

As the Assiniboine River flows into the city of Winnipeg, the last leg of its eastward journey before merging with the Red River, a section of the city known as St. James flanks its northern bank, and it runs past Charleswood and Assiniboine Park to the south. From there, Wellington Crescent, River Heights, and the Osborne Village are on the river's southern shoulder. On its northern bank sits an area called the West End, given that name prior to the municipality of St. James becoming part of Winnipeg—in other words, when it really *was* the west end of the city. The West End turns into downtown after the river runs under the Maryland Bridge.

There are some parks and trails where anyone can access the river, but most riverside property is privately owned. An aerial view shows the river's plethora of meanders; such a winding river offers a lot of riverfront land. When I was growing up and even more so now, those shopping for homes along the river must be prepared to pay premium prices for the privilege of living on the riverbanks. This is a colonial capitalist world view away from the lives of the original Indigenous Peoples, for whom the river was an integral part of their home.

For my ancestors, the river, the land along its banks, and all the life that flourished there were their relatives in the same way that all the other Indigenous nations who traversed the waters and camped on the land were. It was a shared space. The idea of not having access to it, of not being able to put ashore at the best spot for their purposes, the idea of permanent structures disturbing the habitat of creatures whose lives also depended on the river, would have been unimaginable for them. They would have been baffled by a reality in which only the very wealthy could live on the riverbank, with those less well off relegated to only certain spots to go down to the river, as the whole notion of land ownership would have been inconceivable. How could an *anishinaabe*, a human being, own *aki*, the earth, the land?

My street, Strathmillan, was perpendicular to Portage Avenue. At the foot of it, across the eight lanes of Portage, which were bisected by a grassy boulevard, the modern stained glass of St. Paul the Apostle Catholic Church shone in the sunlight of every season from the top of a small hill. The hill was constructed as part of the design; the church "basement" was at ground level around the back. I attended Mass at St. Paul's on Sundays, as well as many events that were held in the basement, including Brownies and Girl Guides.

I don't remember being too bothered by Brownies, but by the time I was old enough to move on to Guides, the paramilitary practices and not-so-subtle social control agenda of these organizations began to irk me. Being indoctrinated with the belief that hierarchy was necessary and good just didn't sit well with me. In fact, recurring themes that spiral through my life are my innate sense of autonomy and independence and my consistent inclination to question authority and the generally accepted ways of doing things that permeate settler colonial culture. Is this the blood memory of my ancestors' resistance to being governed quietly stoking the fire of my feisty spirit?

My friend "Angela" lived one street away from me. Both our mothers were hypercritical and hard on us; our need to get away from them shaped our friendship. When she was ten and I was eleven, we made our first fort together under the front porch of her house. We swept dirt away with a whisk broom, found a scrap of carpet, and fashioned makeshift shelves for the paraphernalia essential to the activities of our secret club. Discarded bathroom tiles lined rough-hewn shelves, which held a cup with a broken handle, a small pad of paper, a pencil, and a deck of cards stored in a rusty tin. There was also a supply of colourful wire sourced from Angela's father, from which we fashioned rings that we sold at school for a quarter apiece. We were saving up for a trip. The flattened side of a cardboard box just inside the opening where we crawled in cut down on the need for sweeping, but we kept the old whisk broom I'd rescued from the garbage there just in case. I remember we had detailed discussions about membership criteria.

We would allow only girls, of course, and we both had to give the stamp of approval for anyone wishing to join. These criteria proved to be stringent enough to ensure we were the only members.

When we found that our first fort was not far enough away from our families, we decided we needed another spot for ourselves. St. Paul's was on riverfront property. The rectory was at the far end of a large parking lot, close to the river and generously shaded by deciduous woods that grew right down to the water. The river near St. Paul's was the perfect spot for a second, more secret fort. I can still see the dirt path through the bush that Angela, also a delinquent Girl Guide, and I followed to get to the fort we made down there. The word *fort* was symbolic by then; our spot was a small clearing by the river. The qualities of a fort that justified the term were the protection and shelter we found there. We had bushwhacked a bit to find it; it wouldn't do for our secret spot to be easily reached by a path others might use.

Every Wednesday after supper, Ange called on me to walk down to Guides together, and on many evenings in the spring and fall, we sauntered right past the doors of the church basement and down to the river. The air was fresh, and the river murmured or chortled, depending on the time of year. Other than that, it was quiet. The cars on Portage Avenue were too far away to be heard, and it was easy to detach from the world we lived in and inhabit our own.

We weren't allowed to go down to the river, of course, which made our secret spot sweeter. The only person who might have observed us was the parish priest, if he happened to be looking out his living room window as we walked by. But he was my paternal uncle John and a maverick in his own right, who toward the end of his career in the priesthood exerted considerable effort to avoid being made a monsignor, having no interest in church bureaucracy. He probably wouldn't have ratted us out.

A few years later, after my younger brother had been unadopted and kicked out, leaving me the sole remaining target for our mother's emotional abuse, my need to leave home became urgent. I turned to Uncle John for help, and he gave me cash from the collection plate, a fistful of five- and ten-dollar bills, enough to buy a plane ticket. Not much discussion—he wasn't much of a talker—just him asking, "How much do you need?" Maybe he'd known about our spot by the river all along.

My memory for details is not good. I don't remember what Angela and I talked about as the river rolled by. But I recall the verdant smell of the muddy bank in the springtime and how our steps raised dust on the dry, hard ground in the fall. And I can always remember the atmosphere, the way times and places in my life felt. I felt I belonged by the river, having found a sense of safety there that was lacking in my white suburban home. I'd breathe deeply, inhaling the distinctive scent of the river like oxygen, knowing in a way that went deeper than all the rules I had to break and the lies I had to tell to be there that I had a right to claim that space.

As long as I stayed close to the river, I wasn't completely lost.

# LOSING ROB THE FIRST TIME

By the time he was a teenager, Rob had grown too big for our mother to hit. I have a stark mental picture of the last time she tried. He grabbed hold of her wrists and held them still, while she flailed and struggled against him, furious and finally powerless. Her ability to get him to do what she wanted was built on a foundation of being able to physically hurt him if he didn't comply; there was no other relationship from which cooperation could flow. Rob and I had experienced enough of our parents' violence by then to have lost respect for them.

After my father came in the door from work that evening, Rob went out to clean the small house trailer that was on blocks in our driveway—the chore he had refused to do earlier, which made our mother lose her temper. He knew he was in trouble and maybe thought if he was doing the chore, it might not be as bad, or maybe he had intended to get it done before Dad got home to avoid being hit but had lost track of time. I see this from the sidewalk on the opposite side of the street. Must've dissociated again. After conferring with my mother, Dad bounded down the few paving stones to the trailer, having completely lost his temper, and just whaled on Rob. The trailer rocked on its blocks, the shocking sound of Rob's screams and cries filling the stagnant air of our supposedly peaceful neighbourhood. It was one of the worst beatings Rob ever endured.

After that, Rob started spending most evenings and nights at the home of a friend, without our parents' permission. He still went to school, but he basically stayed at his friend's house the rest of the time. Our parents constantly told us that our family issues were private, and if we told anyone else about any of it, we were imposing on those people.

In this situation, it was clear that they felt embarrassed by this unwanted exposure. I overheard my dad talking on the phone with the police; he wanted them to go over there and make Rob come home.

I overheard how he related this conversation to our mother: the police had told him that the situation was beyond their purview, because Rob had not committed a crime. The blurring of parental and state authority in my parents' minds still causes me to shake my head. They were incredulous, frustrated that state law enforcement did not extend to the laws they imposed in our home. They did not appreciate being told by the police that their conflict with their son was a "family matter," even though that was precisely what they wanted us to consider it so we would stay silent and carry our family's secrets. Rob's most serious transgression was not staying somewhere other than home; it was breaking that code of silence.

Uncle Derry suggested a family counsellor.

At our parents' request, my older brother and I made ourselves scarce when the counsellor came to the house to meet with Rob and Mom and Dad. I never spoke with Rob about what those sessions were like for him. After three or four of them, my parents asked me to sit in on the next one. I was baffled by this, but they offered no explanation. The counsellor arrived, and I took a seat in our living room, which was decorated straight out of the pages of *Better Homes and Gardens*. The room was furnished with cushy upholstered loveseats and chairs, with glass coffee tables on brass frames sitting atop thick wall-to-wall carpet. Its luxury afforded Rob and me no comfort.

Rob sat in one of the swivel armchairs. I was in a chair right across from him, my eyes fixed on his face. He had the teenage version of the same deer-in-the-headlights look he'd had when he first arrived to live with us. As the session proceeded, it became clear that my role was to be a silent witness. I watched as the counsellor functioned as my parents' mouthpiece, trying to get Rob to see their point of view. That is not family therapy by anyone's definition. At no time did the counsellor create and hold space for Rob to speak or be heard. My heart froze. The two of us sat there as our parents explained, reinforced by the counsellor, that if Rob was not willing to live by their rules, he would be given back to the child welfare agency. They framed this as his choice, downloading the blame for the breakdown of the adoption onto him. He was fifteen years old, trapped in their perception of him as a problem.

To this day, I still wonder why I was asked to be present. Why me and not my older brother, or both of us? It wasn't as though they wanted Rob to have an ally or an advocate to support him, because I wasn't permitted to speak. The only explanation I have been able to come up with is that they wanted to warn me—because from their point of view, I was also a difficult child. This could happen to me too if I didn't toe the line. They needn't have worried. I had been planning my departure for a couple of years by then.

I now understand that the reason I can't remember the days that followed or the actual day Rob moved out is because I was vicariously traumatized by watching this happen. What I do remember is that my brother disappeared, and I was bereft.

Numerous studies have found that the majority of Indigenous transracial adoptions result in negative outcomes. The federal government's Department of Indian Affairs, when that was its name,[5] published statistics revealing that 11,132 First Nations children were adopted between 1960 and 1990. Not accounted for in this figure are hundreds or thousands of Métis children like Rob and me. Indigenous Peoples in Canada include First Nations, Inuit, and Métis, but only First Nations people whose ancestors signed treaties with the colonizers have status. Also not included in that number are the many children whose home communities were not documented in their adoption records. After all, the child welfare agencies and adoptive parents didn't think children like us would ever need that information once the assimilation process had erased all connection to our cultures. Because of this lack of accurate records, Indigenous and settler scholars in the field of Indigenous child welfare agree that the real number of Sixties Scoop adoptees is much higher, now estimated to be at least twenty thousand.[6]

Still, those underestimated stats provide some useful information. For instance, of those eleven-thousand-plus children, 70 percent were placed in white families. And 70 percent of those transracial adoptions broke down. More recent studies cite higher rates of adoption breakdown for Indigenous kids placed in white homes, more like 95 percent, and most of the time it happens when the children become teenagers.[7] Rob and I were not alone. In fact, we were right on schedule.

In Erik Erikson's stages of psychosocial development, the fifth stage occurs between the ages of twelve to eighteen, and it has to do with identity versus role confusion.[8] This is when we ask and try to answer the question "Who am I?" For all teenagers, this is a tumultuous time, accepted as a difficult but necessary part of growing up and taking their place as young adults in a family and a society that offers them a sense of belonging. For Rob and me, with a vast inner void where a feeling of belonging should have been, this was when the general malaise we had felt throughout our childhoods morphed into the acutely painful realization that we were never going to be the people our parents wanted us to be. I don't remember having any positive sense of who I was, only that I was not the daughter my mother wanted, and no amount of effort on my part could change that. I didn't exist beyond the absence of the person I was supposed to be, mirrored back to me in my mother's ever-present disappointment. My self-image was the negative of a photograph.

I have one memory of the effort I made to become a different person. It surfaces every now and then with bittersweet feelings of embarrassment and tenderness toward my teenage self. I thought that if I could change my personality, become a quieter person, I would receive the love and approval I was starving for at home. I would wake up in the morning and resolve not to speak that day unless I was spoken to. I was in grade ten at St. Mary's Academy, a private Catholic girls' school I was expected to attend because my adoptive mother had when she was a young girl. Because all the students travelled there from different parts of the city, we trickled into our classroom one by one as we arrived, well before the bell rang for first class. One morning, when I was trying to be my new, quiet self, my classmates were puzzled. "What's up with Andrea?" one of them asked. "Oh, she's not talking again," another friend answered, her eyes just about rolling right out of her head.

That plan didn't work. By the time the bell rang, I was chatting with the other girls and feeling disappointed in myself. I was trying so hard to find some way to make things better at home. My anguish was my secret.

According to Erikson, getting a sense of who we are in our adolescence is a crucial developmental task, part of developing our sense of self as we head into our adult lives. But there are those of us who have to muddle along without that. The voices of Indigenous people who survived the child welfare system with a shaky or shattered sense of self have been missing in research and literature. This is finally starting to change.

But back then, for my brother Rob and me, in the contest between identity and confusion, confusion always came out the winner.

Rob moved into a group home. It took me a while, but I found him. My sleuthing took a circuitous route; my parents certainly weren't going to tell me where he was. I don't think they knew or cared. Nobody in our family except for me kept in touch with him. Nobody even talked about him at home. It went beyond weird into eerie and scary. It was as if he had died, but in a shameful way, making his name a bad word.

I found out later that during his first night at the group home, he was wakened from his sleep by another resident straddling his chest and threatening him with a knife. Although Rob's life had originated in circumstances similar to those of his new housemates, twelve years in the white suburbs had left him ill-equipped to deal with this. He had to become very tough, very fast.

On the day that I visited him there to bring him a Christmas present, this same boy attacked Rob again. He came into the kitchen, where we were, and asked Rob for a cigarette. Rob handed him a pack, and his housemate took one out. When he handed the pack back to Rob, he flicked it in a way that made all the smokes fall out onto the floor. Rob kept his cool and just asked him to pick them up. The young man exploded and jumped Rob right before my eyes, knocking him to the ground. Staff appeared and tried, without success, to get him off Rob, who was pinned under him, struggling but unable to move. I learned later that this guy had a tendency to flip out like this, and usually the police had to be called and then an ambulance to take him to the hospital, where he would be admitted and sedated.

I was asked to go. The implication was that my visit had caused this, though no further explanation was offered in the heat of the moment. Was Rob's attacker jealous, or just seeking attention? It was gut wrenching to leave my brother so vulnerable, still down on the floor in the midst of a vicious physical attack that even the adults in charge could not stop. Feeling numb, I walked out the door, across the porch, and down the steps in the grey dusk, my solitary footsteps crunching the snow on the walkway.

After that, we met in public places once in a while to catch up, but I never visited Rob at any of his group homes again.

# WARP AND WEFT

surviving my childhood
my first act of resistance

bonding with my baby brother
my first act of solidarity

the first seventeen years of
my life
wove together
forever
my heart and
my passion for
justice

# CHILD ABUSE MATH

I was astonished when I found out that not every kid got hit by their parents. I was in grade eight. I recall being in a daze for a few hours—in class, between classes, while getting something out of my locker. What passed as normal in our house ... wasn't?

I had wondered. One time, I'd threatened to call Children's Aid, and my mom laughed and said ominously, "If you want to call Children's Aid, I'll give you something to call about." I took in that information, and it gave me pause. Not because of her menacing threat, but because it made me wonder if what happened to Rob and me really was abuse.

In child welfare algebra, how much violence equals abuse? We weren't hit every day or even every week. The belittling and being told we were deficient and disappointing was constant though. Does that factor in? What is the metric for emotional abuse? What is its numerical value? Where do I put it in the equation?

What about the nightly whacks on the butt from our mother as part of her ritual of tucking us in? Every single night, for years, she would come into our rooms after we were in bed, fuss with the covers a little, make the sign of the cross on our foreheads, then hit us on the behind. She called it a "love pat," but it *hurt*. How much does that add to the account? Does the pairing of hitting with making the sign of the cross count for more?

Even after I had left home, whenever I came back to visit, she would do this. I am embarrassed and ashamed to disclose that I was in my twenties before I summoned up the courage to tell her to stop. That I didn't like it and didn't want her to do it ever again. She appeared hurt and said I was making a big deal about nothing, but she agreed. On which side of the equation does *that* belong?

A friend was once reading over my writing, giving me feedback. "Your childhood was so violent."

Was it? The physical violence was sporadic. The emotional abuse was unrelenting. The danger was constant. We never felt safe.

When does the equation stop mattering because the fear has reached the nth degree and gone exponential?

# NIIZHOZIIBEAN—TWO RIVERS IV

The Assiniboine River flows southeast through St. James, toward its rendezvous with the Red River in the centre of the city. In the summer, canoe enthusiasts paddle past grassy banks under overhanging maples, gliding by sandy beaches on the lower flats. At certain times of the year, the water may be shallow and low relative to the banks. In late summer, when the foliage is at its fullest, those paddlers would be hard pressed to see or hear any sign of a world beyond the river.

Except for the bridges encountered along the way.

There are forty-three vehicular bridges within Winnipeg city limits. Five of these—the Charleswood Bridge, the St. James Bridge, the Maryland Bridge, the Osborne Street Bridge, and the Midtown Bridge (commonly known as the Donald Street Bridge)—along with the Assiniboine Park Footbridge, span the Assiniboine. Experienced paddlers know to be careful of potentially hazardous currents around bridge pillars and to take extra care when passing underneath. There are also small islands and late-season sandbars, variations in the world of the river that paddlers must watch for, as any deviations in the river's path complicate the currents.

Travelling through this green corridor, paddlers are serenaded by songbirds singing in the trees along the banks, the odd kingfisher, and sometimes geese overhead.

I travelled on the river for transportation once.

I went to St. Mary's Academy for grades seven through ten. The bus ride there from our house, including one transfer, took about an hour and fifteen minutes. I took the bus home every day but was not expected to in the mornings. Instead, I could get a ride to school with my dad on his way to work downtown.

In the spring and fall, I often rode my bike back and forth to St. Mary's. I'd ride along Bruce Avenue as far as Overdale Street to avoid the eight lanes of traffic on Portage Avenue, walk my bike across Portage at the lights, then ride over the footbridge, through Assiniboine Park to Wellington Crescent and along the southern bank of the river the rest of the way to school.

Sometime during my high school years, I fell in love with cross-country skiing. I also loved going on adventures and had no hesitation about going alone when companions were not readily available. One winter's day, I cross-country skied to and from school. I packed my homework and lunch in a backpack and dressed in my ski gear and boots. My uniform was in my locker at school, so I didn't have to carry a change of clothes. I don't recall any conversation about this plan at home, but my parents would obviously have known I was doing this; it would have been hard to miss.

It was a crisp Winnipeg winter morning. I carried my skis and poles over my shoulder as I walked down to the river, then clipped on my skis a short step down the bank, at the spot where Ange and I had hung out when we were skipping out of Girl Guides. I could see my breath in the pale-blue morning air.

I set off, staying close to the north bank. If for some reason I had to stop, I wanted to be somewhere it would be easy to get home from on foot. This was before the days of cellphones and helicopter parents. I don't recall making any kind of backup plan with my mother. In this memory, like many from my childhood, I am solitary, almost as if I lived alone.

I fell into the easy rhythm of the skiing, cross-currents of energy streaming through me, effort and motion in perfect symmetry. While not athletically inclined in any of the competitive sports that were forced on us in phys. ed. class, I had stamina. In my experience, stamina is a spiritual as well as physical thing. Even today, when biking up a long, challenging hill, I repeat a mantra in my mind that grounds me in the knowledge that my body is not my spirit, and though my body might be struggling, my spirit is doing fine. More often than not, that shift in awareness is enough to overcome the protests of my loudly complaining muscles and get me to the top without having to dismount and walk my bike.

Finding my groove in skiing that day, I covered kilometre after kilometre in Zenlike, silent meditation. The sound of my breath played a percussive duet with the swishing sound of my skis sliding over the snow-covered river.

I passed underneath the Assiniboine Park Footbridge, which I'm guessing was about one-third of the way there. Not too much farther along, I passed under the St. James Bridge. When I reached the Maryland Bridge, I had to scout for a place to take my skis off and scramble up the steep bank to the intersection of Academy Road and Wellington Crescent. Funny that I don't have a clear memory of that—it was probably the most challenging part. What I do remember is the fine feeling of accomplishment as I crossed Wellington and Academy at the lights and walked into school with my skis and poles balanced on my right shoulder.

I propped my skis and poles in a corner of the locker room, out of the way, then joined in the chatter of teenage girls changing into their uniforms and gathering up their books. Just another day at school.

At the end of the school day, I retraced my steps and had the benefit of skiing back home on the track I had made in the morning. I had a moment of anxiety when I found myself skiing through a slushy section, the natural result of a day of sunshine in late winter. The endorphins released by the exercise balanced out the adrenalin surge, and I had a clear thought: if I skied closer to the bank and kept a watchful eye, there was every reason to believe I could make it home, and if not, I'd be close enough to land to be able to walk up and find a place to rest before my wet feet froze. I was in the middle of the city, after all, not alone in the wilderness.

I made it home, a warm glow radiating through me. I put my skis and poles away in the basement and then took out my homework, my unique expedition blending into the regular weekday routine. I was happy to have spent a good part of my day on the river. What I didn't know was that I had retraced a route travelled by my ancestors thousands of years, hundreds of years, and decades before me. Perhaps, like them, I got a whiff of freedom from these solitary adventures. The faint scent of it sustained me.

The late April sun beat down on the sidewalk where my friend Ellen and I sat side by side, our backs leaning against the warm stone of the Canadian National Railway station on Main Street. Winnipeg Transit buses heaved and belched as they left the bus stop close by us and headed for North Main, where, unbeknownst to me, my birth family brothers and sisters were hanging out in the city's urban Indigenous community. This neighbourhood is sometimes called the largest reserve in Canada, as the majority of Winnipeg's over ninety thousand Indigenous residents live there. If I had known them then, I might not have come to the conclusion that there was nothing for me in Winnipeg, but things being what they were, I was waiting to board a train that would take me as far away as possible.

The train station in Winnipeg is located right where the two rivers meet—Niizhoziibean, the Forks. There, where my history reaches back many generations, I was embarking on a journey that would take me away from those as yet unknown origins, as well as the ones I knew far too well: the heartbreak that had come to define my experience of family up to that point.

Ellen had come to see me off. I had told her it wasn't necessary, but she had insisted. She skipped school and borrowed her family's car to pick me up at Camp Manitou, where I was living and working, and drive me downtown to the station. She was in her last semester of grade twelve at Silver Heights Collegiate.

I had left the same school after the fall semester, having planned my courses so I could complete grades eleven and twelve in a year and a half. I was determined to get away as soon as I could. By the end of December, I had one-and-a-half credits left to complete. It should have been only a half credit, but I had quit math, a subject I had always found difficult. I convinced my parents that I should not attend school for that last semester because, with only a couple of classes, I would have too much time on my hands and might get into trouble. Playing into this stereotype-based myth about youth worked. I found a job as part of the maintenance crew at Camp Manitou, a YMCA camp in Headingly, on the western outskirts of the city. Camp Manitou was just far enough away to be beyond the city transit routes, so I had to live there. My mother had not hesitated to give her permission; I'm sure she was glad to have me out of the house.

Once I moved out in January, my preparations to leave for good began in earnest.

I saved as much money as I could. I had another close friend, a guy four years older than me. When my hope that we could be more than friends did not pan out, I had one less reason to stay and decided it was time to get out of town. Contrary to the ever-popular desire to go west, I was intrigued by the Atlantic coast, simply because it was a total mystery to me. In my experience, when people from Winnipeg said "out east," they usually meant Toronto. Those with a more expansive sense of our country might think of Montreal, but almost never Quebec City. The Atlantic provinces just didn't exist in the consciousness of the people I grew up around. That was why it appealed to me; the region was a complete unknown. What better place to discover another complete unknown—myself?

My final destination was Halifax, but I thought it was too risky to go there right away. I had an aunt who lived in Halifax, and I had to stay on the down-low until I turned eighteen, the age of majority in Manitoba. Once I was eighteen, my parents wouldn't be able to force me to come home.

I had purchased a train ticket to Fredericton under an assumed name. I chuckle at this now. Seems odd that I wasn't asked for ID when I picked up the ticket I had booked over the phone—but I wasn't. I'd stepped up to the wicket, my heart in my throat, and been given my ticket, no questions asked. I was seventeen and about to travel halfway across the country without my parents' knowledge or permission. Ticket in hand, Grandma's hard-sided suitcase and my guitar on one side of me and Ellen on the other, I sat on the sidewalk outside the station waiting for my train, feeling calm.

My friend, on the other hand, was crying. She was the only person I'd told that I was leaving and where I was going. I warned her that my parents would call the police, who would probably question her. (This happened as I had predicted, and she was called out of class to speak to police officers but told them nothing.) When the time came for me to head to the platform, we hugged, and I promised to call her as soon as I was settled. I had already bought a phone card, so I was all set. I had $400 in my wallet; that would have to last until I found a job and got my first paycheque.

I stowed my suitcase and guitar in the luggage area and settled into my seat. I felt no grief. I was peaceful. I'd known soul-deep aloneness for a long time by then. Forced to become emotionally independent at a young age, to me physical independence felt like a walk in the park by comparison. I had written letters to my parents, my two grandmothers, and a couple of other people and mailed them earlier that day.

I was ready. The train hummed and chuffed, gathering the energy to get itself moving down the track, and then we were off. On family drives back from the lake, we used to be able to see the Winnipeg sky-line when we were still at least a half-hour from the city. Its downtown skyscrapers rose up from the flatlands, looking like little LEGO towers from a distance.

On that day, I did not glance back.


An unexpected bonus: I discovered a lifelong love of trains.

I had never been on a train trip before, and my initiation was intense: five days and four nights in the cheap seats. Back then, I was open to meeting people. Anything and everyone new was welcome. Now when I travel coach, I try to be one of the first to board so I can spread my stuff out on the seats across from me and put my earbuds in so I don't have to lie when other passengers ask me if those seats are taken, a play for solitude that sometimes works. But on my very first train ride, I was interested in meeting people. It didn't take long.

An Acadian man in his late twenties had noticed that I had a guitar with me. He approached me and, in his few English words and my high school French, we talked. His name was Jean Claude, and he was a professional guitar player, a session musician who had played on recordings and in live shows with the well-known Québécoise chanteuse Ginette Reno. Jean Claude was an amazing guitarist, and it was a treat to hear him play my guitar, getting sounds out of it that I had never heard before.

He was going home to Tracadie, New Brunswick, so we would be travelling companions for the whole trip. Both of us had to disembark at the same station in Chatham-Newcastle, two towns right next to each other that are now called Miramichi for the beautiful river that flows through the area. There were no passenger trains that went to Fredericton, so my ticket included bus fare for the last leg of the trip.

As we approached Montreal, where we would have a layover of several hours, Jean Claude told me that when we got there, he was going to a friend's apartment, for which he had a key, to grab a shower. He asked if I wanted to come along. I knew this was a risky business and gave it some thought. After three nights of sleeping on the train, washing up in the tiny bathroom sink was not cutting it. My naïveté and intense longing for the feeling of hot water cascading over me won out, and I accepted the invitation. We were switching trains at the Gare Centrale, so we took our luggage with us. On what was my first subway ride, I was encumbered with a guitar and a suitcase. Jean Claude had only one bag, so he carried my guitar, and it wasn't too bad. I was intrigued by Montreal and decided to add it to the list of places I would go in my travels. A little over a year later, I kept that promise to myself and took a bus to Montreal from California and lived there for several months.

But that day, Montreal's appeal was all about getting clean. We arrived at the apartment, a hole in the wall in a nondescript building, small but cozy. Everything went according to plan until Jean Claude made his move. He wanted to have sex. I expressed a very valid concern about getting back in time to catch our train. I had no intention of having sex with him. I liked this guy, but not enough to mess up my plans. He respected my boundaries, and we set off.

I like to think that I have good radar for reading people. Throughout my life, I have been able to find a balance between openness and caution. But when I think of that year and a half and all the situations I was in that could have been catastrophic, I have to believe that I was being protected. It is said that when we take a step in the right direction, the universe conspires to help us. My life is a testament to this. Leaving home when I did was the most important step I have ever taken. I was guided by Creator to take that step and protected through all the steps that followed.

Jean Claude and I nearly missed our train. We sprinted through the station, him carrying my guitar, and we were out of breath as we climbed the steps into our car at the very last minute. Once we were settled in, we laughed long and hard. All's well that ends well.

Until that epic trip, the only time I'd ridden the rails was on a miniature train through Assiniboine Park as a child. On that first real train trip, lulled by the sounds and the swaying of the cars rolling down the tracks, day and night for the better part of a week, I fell in love with trains. In subsequent years, in gaps between train rides, I kept this love alive by singing about them. I learned Emmylou Harris's version of "Hobo's Lullaby" years ago, and it's still a favourite. In the mid-1980s, when I lived with a family who had a toddler, a child who became a permanent part of my family, I learned the song "Morningtown Ride," a Malvina Reynolds tune first released in 1966. As the years went on, Birds of Chicago's "Time and Times" and Kasey Chambers's "Runaway Train" made it on to my set lists. One time, at a jam session with a bunch of musicians at my house, I cracked everyone up when a friend was giving us a rendition of "City of New Orleans," and I snuck a wooden train whistle out of my basket of percussion instruments and blew it right on time with the lyrics. Rail fan, rail buff, train buff, trainspotter—whatever you want to call it, I'm one of those.

When I was pregnant with my child, the idea that babies in the womb can hear the music we sing and listen to resonated with me. Some say that the songs babies hear before they are born can comfort them once they arrive in the world, because the sound is so familiar to them. My experience bore this out. I sang "Hobo's Lullaby" and "Morningtown Ride" to my unborn child more often than any other songs. And sure enough, whenever I sang these songs to Rowan in his infancy, he was soothed.

I don't know if I instilled a love of trains in my child. I took him on a few train trips, starting when he was small enough to stretch out and sleep comfortably on a coach seat. He is all grown up and living in Kjipuktuk (Halifax) now, and I don't know if there are more train rides in his future. I do know he has fallen in love with Montreal.

Chugging by la ville de Quebec in the middle of the night and seeing it from across the river in Lévis was one of my favourite experiences on the train—on that first trip and many times since. Built in 1893, Château Frontenac and the promenade in front of it were lit by warm light from old-fashioned street lamps. These lights, in turn, reflected down a dark, steep bank below onto the moving surface of the St. Lawrence River. It was magical.

Later that morning, we arrived in Newcastle, a quaint little town bathed in spring sun. Jean Claude gave me his address, and I promised to write. I would catch my bus later that afternoon at the train station, so I stowed my luggage behind the ticket counter and set off to explore the town. I bought a copy of the Fredericton *Daily Gleaner* and found a great little diner. I slid into the cherry-red vinyl seat of a booth and spread out the Classifieds section on the matching red laminate table, my bacon and eggs and mug of coffee off to the side. Scanning the ads, I circled rooms for rent and potential jobs.

An unfamiliar mix of excitement and perfect contentment coursed through me.

*I was free.*

# Interlude

# WHEN SHE WAS WHITE

when she was white
she smiled as best she could
tilting her head to one side
in every photograph
making her body into
a question
mark

when she was white
she peered through the
slats of her solitude at
the planet
she had
landed on

she prepared to
retrace her steps
what she needed was
easy to carry
her story
her song
her medicine
truth
revealed to her by
its absence
in the cracks
in the hard earth a
parched
silence

as soon as she left
her Spirit Guides began to
appear
on trains they let her nestle
into their shoulders and sleep
in boarding houses they stared at her over
cups of strong tea, the
canned milk making
sticky rings on the vinyl tablecloth.

they gave her rides home in their
police cars
they let her stay with them in their
convents
they sunned themselves next to her on
beaches
and sat beside her on
long Greyhound bus rides

they refracted the little light she needed and
steadied her

as she dangled in the dark space
between two worlds

# III

# A REGRETTABLE
# UNFORGETTABLE CHRISTMAS

Sometime in my early twenties, in what hindsight would say was against my better judgment, I caved in to pressure from my adoptive family to come home for Christmas. I remember only one part of that trip home, and it's the one part I wish I could forget.

Christmas dinner was, as always, a meal we ate in the dining room at a beautiful and rarely used mahogany table set with a white linen tablecloth, the good china and silver, and the silver salt and pepper set. The saltcellar had a round royal-blue glass insert and what I always thought was the sweetest tiny silver spoon to serve oneself some salt with. Because salt was never to be sprinkled directly onto the food— far too gauche for a formal dinner—but instead deposited in a genteel little mound at the edge of the plate, for dipping a forkful of food in. The shape of the matching pepper shaker echoed the architecture of the Eastern Orthodox churches on North Main; the midsection was cinched in and then swelled into a tiny dome at the top that looked like a poppy pod ready to burst.

We all dressed up for Christmas dinner, and as always, I was seated to the right of my adoptive mother so I could be called upon to refill serving dishes or fetch other things from the kitchen as needed. As the only girl in the family, I had specific duties that were made clear in my mother's very deliberate training of me as a hostess.

That year, my good outfit was a cotton peasant dress with beige leggings. In my early twenties, I was a young feminist who had sworn off pantyhose and other dictates of the feminine fashion of the day that I equated with sexism and a lack of freedom of expression for women. I wore clothes I could feel comfortable in—what a concept! It didn't take much to be a revolutionary in that household. I don't remember what I wore on my feet in the house, probably nothing, but when I went outdoors, the dressy look was completed by a pair of sturdy hiking boots, much to my mother's bare-faced disgust.

To be fair, I was not trying to offend or irk anyone. This was simply the way I dressed at that time. In my circle of loved ones and friends on the east coast, I was considered attractive, and I would have received compliments on my outfit. Dressing this way at home that Christmas, I was just choosing not to put on a costume and perform.

It was a small group of us for Christmas dinner that year. My adoptive parents sat at either end of the formal dining table; my gran on my dad's left; my older brother's fiancée on my dad's right; and my older brother next to her, across from me. My mother's mother had died shortly after I left home, and Rob was no longer part of the family.

Although my older brother has long since outgrown this behaviour, at that time he took great pleasure in baiting me about what everyone there considered my radical views. Against the white-bread backdrop of middle-class suburbia, it didn't take much to be labelled a rebel. He came at me in between first and second helpings, laughed condescendingly about my clothes, and attributed to me every negative cliché about feminists that he could think of—no need to repeat them here. It made me uncomfortable, of course, but I kept silent as he continued to throw his verbal darts. Eventually, I made a comment suggesting he might want to educate himself a bit about the issues before taking an anti-feminist position. The mildest of retorts, but still too much for this family.

My mother raised her wineglass and called for a toast. "To Andrea," she said. "May she come often and never stay too long."

There was stunned silence.

Broken by my father, who, bless his heart, was shocked by his wife's cold comment. "Duckie!" he exclaimed, using his term of endearment for her, though he was genuinely taken aback.

And what did I say?

Nothing. Seconds ticked by.

Then, I fawned. The concept of fawning as a trauma response is a recent addition to the previously understood trauma responses of fight, flight, or freeze. The term was coined by psychotherapist Pete Walker and refers to situations in which a person facing conflict or danger tries to "pacify, please, and cater to the needs of others, rather than their own."[9]

Did I state the obvious, that it was clear I had already stayed too long, then stand up, leave the table, gather my things from my old room, and call a friend to come and pick me up? Not that time, although I did escape that way from another painful visit. Did I call out my mother's rudeness? No. Do I wish now that I had done either or both of those things? Of course. The woman I later became, the woman I am now, does not tolerate being treated with disrespect, let alone cruelty.

But that day, I calmly turned to my father and said, "It's all right, Dad. At least I know where I stand." And continued to eat the now tasteless plate of food in front of me.

Freeing oneself from learned helplessness is a long process.

# BLOOD MEMORY

Blood memory ... is an invisible connection with something that surprises and mystifies you ... [It] relates to behaviours that have not been taught, but that people exhibit or feel. The Aboriginal people absolutely believe that humans are born understanding or knowing certain things and that through sharing beliefs, modelling ideals, rituals and ceremonies this information that is already in the person's subconscious mind is unlocked and become conscious. This consciousness includes spirituality, responsibility, reciprocity, the earth, animals and many other facets of life.
—NOLA TURNER-JENSEN [10]

One time when we were at Netley Creek, in the low-budget cottage my parents had built from plywood and insulated with busted-up cardboard boxes, I harvested an armful of reeds and wove a mat. I had never made one before and was pleased with how it turned out, although the weave loosened as the yellowing fronds dried. Dad looked at it with admiration and asked, "Where did you learn how to do that?" I had no idea. It had just come into my head as something I wanted to do.

◆●◆

"Blood memory" is the idea that we carry ancient memories in our DNA, genetic connections to the teachings of our ancestors, and that these memories can be awakened.
—Exploring "Blood Memory" | INDIGENOUS FORUM [11]

◆●◆

Out at Netley, we often went fishing in a small aluminum boat that started out with a five-horsepower motor and moved on to more powerful motors in increments over the years. Dad occupied the driver's seat at the stern, my brothers and I had the middle seat, and Mom was in the bow seat with Penny, our dog. We'd putter through the marsh, spending the better part of the day on the water. I did not cognitively know at that time that this marsh was a crucial part of my ancestral territory, a network of waterways my people used for harvesting food and for travel. I just loved being in the midst of it.

Once we decided on a spot and lowered the homemade anchor—an old cooking pot filled with cement—we were immersed in the marsh's rich life. Lily pads and water skimmers, frogs and dragonflies, gulls and crows. Sometimes red-winged blackbirds. Ducks, of course. There were lots of fish. I remember catching perch and bass, the odd pickerel, and pike. The pike, which we also called jackfish, were huge in my little girl's eyes. And every now and then we'd reel in a catfish and marvel at its long, white whiskers before letting it go.

My brothers would grow bored while we waited for a nibble on our lines. They wanted action, and they wanted it *now*. But I could sit in the boat for hours, quiet and content. The gifts and teachings of fishing are numerous; it's not just about catching fish. It's about being on or near the water, tuning in to all the life below the surface, hanging out on the border between the elements of water and air. It is contemplative and also, just fishing.

I asked Dad to teach me how to fillet the fish. After that, I was often the one who cleaned them. The whole process of harvesting food from the wild, preparing it for consumption, and eating it, in all its fresh goodness, gave me such peace.

●–●–●

Blood memory is described as our ancestral (genetic) connection to our language, songs, spirituality, and teachings. It is the good feeling that we experience when we are near these things.

—ZIIBIWING CENTER[12]

One day, when I was a teenager, we were all sitting down at the dinner table when the doorbell rang. I got up to answer it while my mother and father and two brothers stayed at the table. I opened the door to see two young boys of about ten or eleven. They were asking for a donation of food. I let them step inside and went to the pantry cupboard in the kitchen, a set of six shelves containing mostly tins and non-perishables. That cupboard was always full; it represented to me an unending supply of food. I always knew that we would never go without. As I picked out a couple of cans of soup and spaghetti to give to the boys, my father asked who was at the door. I explained that two young boys had asked for food, and my dad told me to stop what I was doing.

"We have no idea who they are, or if they are really in need. Did they say what organization they're working with? Did they show you any identification?"

"No," I said, "they just asked if I had any food."

"Well, you are not to give them anything. Go and tell them we're not able to help at this time."

I stood frozen on the spot in utter disbelief. First of all, going door to door asking for food couldn't be very high on the list of pranks a couple of young boys up to good would want to pull. And second, even if they weren't genuinely in need, we would only be out a couple of cans of food that we wouldn't even miss. Why not err on the side of generosity?

I couldn't go back to the boys and send them away empty handed—I didn't have the heart. I sat back down in my seat at the table and told my dad that he would have to tell them. Which he did, looking disgruntled when he came back.

Years later, while visiting with my oldest biological sister, we were sharing stories from our separate childhoods. I was describing the affluence I had grown up in and how it had sometimes made me feel acutely uncomfortable, and I told her this story as an example.

She stated simply, "You were thinking like a Métis."

My birth mother reinforced this while telling me about her life on the trapline with her first husband. Although she sometimes went out to check the traps with him on their dogsled, she did not go every time, so sometimes she was alone in their cabin in the bush for weeks at a time. She explained to me that if anyone arrived at the cabin, be they friend or stranger, the custom was to feed them a good meal, no questions asked, before they went on their way again. This was about survival, a practice that ensured that anyone out on the land and in need of food would be able to eat at the first house they came upon. A person could never know when they might be the one in need.

This idea was further emphasized for me years later, when I read an article about Métis economics and how economic security for us was based on a tradition of sharing rather than acquiring. The author included a teaching from a Métis Elder who said that, dating back to before our people had electricity, "the best ice box for your game is in the stomach of your neighbours."[13] Sharing was an expression of our interconnectedness, but it was also about food security for everyone.

●●●

Blood memory ... only becomes detectable when one culture's assumptions, rules and unspoken values about the way things should work, are confronted with another culture who holds a polar opposite set of assumptions and rules and unspoken values.

—NOLA TURNER-JENSEN[14]

●●●

I was standing on the northeast corner of Portage Avenue and Sherbrooke Street, waiting for the transfer bus that would take me the rest of the way home from high school. It was a bitterly cold Winnipeg winter afternoon, with a cutting westerly wind making me burrow my face into the scarf I wore around my neck. The rest of me was toasty warm in a hand-me-down coat from my mother that I loved. Its thick grey wool covered me from my neck down to the middle of my calves, in the midi style of the seventies. It was a garment of high quality, made by the English company Niccolini, and it had a sharp-looking cape that buttoned on under the collar and came down well past my shoulders. I had always admired this coat whenever my mother wore it, and it was the only article of clothing she ever gave me that I really loved. (I'm not the only one; the internet is full of vintage Niccolini coats. They are still in demand.) I was aware the coat was high end, but it was the warmth it offered that made it my choice on those frigid winter days when I'd have to stand out in the wind and snow, waiting for my bus.

As I nuzzled into my warm coat in the extreme cold that afternoon, three Indigenous children came careening around the corner from Sherbrooke, heading east on the icy sidewalk. All three of them wore tattered sneakers with plastic bags in them to help keep their feet dry, even though the bags would make their feet sweat and leave them even more susceptible to freezing. All of a sudden, I was acutely aware of the opulent coat I was wearing, and an unbidden thought came to my mind: *That could be me.*

This memory is seared into my psyche, as are many other random moments of unexplainable insight. I don't know how I knew this or how I analyzed what the thought could mean. I just had a strong feeling that only by chance was I the one with the warm coat on; it could just as easily have been me with the plastic bag–lined sneakers.

●●●

In psychology, genetic memory is defined as a memory present at birth that exists in the absence of sensory experience and is incorporated into the genome over long spans of time. In everyday terms, that means we remember things that we have never been exposed to, because it's been in our genes for so long.
—NOLA TURNER-JENSEN[15]

●●●

At the same time that I was sorting through and writing these stories, I was reading and watching webinars about different Indigenous teachings, and the concept of blood memory kept coming up. One such occasion was during an online session about medicine bundles that Anishinaabe Elder Barb Cameron offered a group of us Indigenous therapists. Barb is second-degree Midewiwin. (The Midewiwin Lodge is sometimes referred to in English as the Grand Medicine Society; the most accurate translation is "spiritual mystery.") Memories I had never fully understood were surfacing, and I needed to know more. I offered tobacco to Barb and asked her to teach me about blood memory. She generously shared her knowledge with me:

"Blood memory is carried in our bodies. All of a sudden, you know how to do something you have never done before, and you have no idea how you know. You are carrying the blood of your ancestors, all those who came before you that you are connected to. They survived a great deal, and they knew how to live on much less. They had knowledge of astronomy and other sciences, mathematics, and geography. The truth is, we carry that knowledge. When things come to you, it's not by chance. That knowledge is part of you. It came from somewhere! We call that blood memory."

◆◆◆

Monarch butterflies each year make a 2,500-mile journey from Canada to a small plot of land in Mexico where they winter. In spring they begin the long journey back north, but it takes three generations to do so. So no butterfly making the return journey has flown that entire route before.
—DAROLD TREFFERT[16]

◆◆◆

If a monarch butterfly who has never seen their summer home knows how to get there, maybe I can find my way home too.

Maybe that's what I've been doing all along.

# NIIZHOZIIBEAN—TWO RIVERS V

When they left the larger Sioux Nation and branched off on their own, the Assiniboine carried with them a dialect of the Sioux language known as Nakota, but they and their Sioux relatives did not part on good terms. The Sioux referred to the Assiniboine as the *Hohe*,[17] and for years, there were skirmishes between them. The Assiniboine ended up forming an alliance with the Woodland Cree, their neighbours to the northeast, who assisted in battles against the Dakota. As they paddled on the Assiniboine River in those days, *otôsim*, their canoes, would have been ready for war.

The Red River that flows through the life of my family has two parts: the Red River of the south, which is part of the Mississippi-Missouri river system, and the Red River of the north. It flows north due to the gradual downhill slope between its place of origin and its ultimate destination, Hudson Bay. The Red River grows deeper and wider as it gathers in the Pembina and Roseau rivers before being joined by the Assiniboine at Niizhoziibean. At its widest, it is eighty kilometres across. I hadn't known how deep an impression the rivers of my childhood had made on me until I came to Nova Scotia and saw the rivers here—to my mind, they were mere creeks. In New Brunswick, when I first saw the Saint John River flowing through Fredericton on its way to the Bay of Fundy, I thought, *Now* that's a *river*.

Before it reaches Niizhoziibean, the Red River passes through the rural towns of St. Jean Baptiste, Morris, Ste. Agathe, and St. Adolphe.

A Métis settlement since before 1812, St. Adolphe is where my birth mother was born and grew up. The town was home then to about five hundred people. It sits on the eastern bank of the Red River and was evacuated twice, during the floods of 1950 and 1966. In those floods, my family's home literally was the Red River.

My grandfather, Joe Courchaine, worked as a bridge-builder and a market gardener. My grandmother, Marie Thérèse Goulet Courchaine, was a schoolteacher who worked away from home while Maman, my two aunts, and my uncle attended the Roman Catholic boarding school that had been established in St. Adolphe by the Filles de la Croix in 1906. The nuns were not Métis, and the atmosphere at the school was harsh, the discipline severe. It is considered to have been one of the many non-registered Indian residential schools in Canada. My mother's stories of her time there blur in my mind with the many stories of residential school survivors I have heard throughout my years working in Indigenous mental health and healing in Mi'kma'ki. My mother was considered a residential school survivor, and in the later years of her life, when she was actively involved in the Manitoba Métis Federation, she attended healing gatherings with other survivors in our homeland.

In the summer of 1998, having just met Maman, I went to St. Adolphe with her and Auntie Pat.

First, we visited the convent school on the main drag of the town, situated on the same property as the St. Adolphe Roman Catholic Church and Cemetery. Maman and my auntie didn't say too much about what it was like when they were students there. Most residential school survivors I have spoken with have told me that they were primarily a source of free labour at their school, and their learning was secondary to that work. When I asked Maman if they had had any chores, she told me that she had to clean the stairs, a little girl going from step to step on her knees, up and down the huge institutional staircases.

Grandpa Joe is buried in the cemetery there, so we visited his grave. I tried to speak to him in my heart. He is much more remote to me than his vivacious wife, my indomitable grandma Marie Thérèse. She was a writer of renown; much has been written about her. He is harder to get to know. Standing in reflective silence by his grave, I greeted him, explained who I was, and told him that I wished I could have met him before he died, that I was sure there was so much he could have taught me. That I wished I could have worked beside him in his garden. I am trying to garden these days, but not having grown up around much gardening, there's a lot of trial and error. Later that day, Maman gave me my grandpa's rosary beads, which he'd cherished—and now, so do I.

Then we found the grassy field where their childhood home had once stood. Arms stretching out to indicate areas of the land within sight, my mother and her sister sketched out the perimeter walls of the house and showed me where the huge garden had been.

The writer Gabrielle Roy had been a frequent visitor to that house, as she was a good friend of my grandmother's. Grandma's success as a writer was in no small way due to the encouragement of Madame Roy. My mother had been a little girl then, and she remembered those visits, telling me about the chair Madame Roy always sat in, rubbing her thumbs on its wooden arms and eventually leaving permanent grooves in the wood.

My biological sister's happiest childhood memories are her summertime visits with Grandma in that house. Life with our mother had been chaotic, to say the least. At Grandma's house in St. Adolphe, my sister felt special, well cared for, and secure.

As Maman and Auntie Pat reminisced about their childhood, trying to figure out whose bedroom was on which patch of weedy grass, I felt my roots rise up to greet me through the warm earth beneath my feet.

If I made a random squiggle drawing and coloured in the closed spaces with a green pencil crayon, the result would be a close approximation of an aerial view of Netley Marsh. Our family's cottage is located along one of the lines connecting those green spots, on Netley Creek, one of the marsh's waterways that winds along its northern edge before emptying into the southern end of Lake Winnipeg. Fish and birds abound.

The creek bottom is soft mud, so to get into the water without feeling mud oozing between their toes, cottagers have to truck in gravel and sand to make their own little beaches. Once you're out deep enough, you can forget what's at the bottom—unless you jump off the end of the dock, feet first. I did this often as a kid, my feet feeling the mud and its ominous contents with a split-second thrill that propelled me back up to the surface like a shot.

The cottage passed from our family to both of my dad's brothers in turn. The story goes like this: Dad "sold" the cottage to Uncle John, who, as a Catholic priest, had very little disposable income. Whatever Uncle John did have, he spent on sailboats, starting with a little rowboat with a drop keel and a holder in the hull where a mast could go—his first boat, bought from Eaton's for a few hundred dollars. Whenever he was sailing, he could shed being Father Currie and just be John, an affable skipper blending in with everyone else, tinkering with his boat or reading the winds. Apparently, Dad gave him a really good deal on the cottage, the charitable act of a good Catholic. After a few upgrades to bigger and bigger sailboats, Uncle John flipped the cottage to Uncle Derry, who had ended up with the lion's share of social conscience in that family and would never dream of paying a family member any less than what the cottage was worth. Uncle John made a handsome profit, enough to buy himself a gorgeous twenty-six-foot full-keel offshore ocean sailboat, which he had for the rest of his life. Dad never quite got over this, although he enjoyed many happy days crewing for Uncle John on the sturdy sloop, which was christened *Up the Creek*.

I kept in touch with Rob for two years after he was kicked out of our family and up until I left on my travels. One of the group homes he lived in was in the Silver Heights Collegiate school district; when I was in grade twelve there, he was in grade ten—that is, when he showed up. Once, when his absences accrued to the point that he was going to be expelled, I went to the principal to advocate for him, explaining his circumstances and promising to help him with his schoolwork. I did this in consultation with Rob only; our parents knew nothing about his situation or my efforts on his behalf. The principal relented and let Rob stay. Rob went back to attending his classes, but it was short lived. He was kicked out and never passed grade ten.

After I left town, I looked him up every couple of years, whenever I visited Winnipeg. On one of those trips, I attended Rob's wedding. In fact, I went with our adoptive mother and father and older brother, whom Rob had invited. Rob had kept in touch sporadically with our adoptive parents. I believe he just thought that they should be there. By then, he had been excluded from extended family gatherings for years; other than me, he had no other family to invite. I was as happy as ever to see him, although being at the wedding with the rest of our adoptive family was awkward, to say the least. Our parents did not approve of Rob's choice—a feisty woman whom I really liked—and they and our older brother were stiff and uncomfortable throughout the day. At the reception in a community hall, the four of us appeared to be the only ones not having fun. I remember wanting to cross the floor and go party with my new in-laws, but I was unwilling to deal with the drama that would have caused. Just before we left, Dad went to speak with the father of the bride. When he returned, he informed us that he had paid for the liquor. I guess when no shared understanding or genuine connection exists, money can stand in as a substitute for love and support.

I visited Rob and his wife in Winnipeg—until he decided that my ongoing, albeit ambivalent and strained, relationship with our parents made me untrustworthy. After that he dropped off my radar as well. For a period of about ten years, I didn't know where or how he was. It was another layer of loss I carried, a shadowy grief haunting the edges of my late twenties and early thirties. Thoughts of Rob were always there, on the periphery of my awareness.

Once, at a cabin in Pictou County, a song about Rob came to me out of nowhere. When I had finished composing it, I played it for my girl-friend, releasing many years' worth of tears that drenched the summer afternoon. Then the grief sank out of sight once more, nestling back into its subliminal home.

It didn't arise again until a couple of years later, when I was on a meditation retreat at Gampo Abbey in the Cape Breton highlands. While I was sitting on my cushion in the shrine room, my grief about Rob surfaced as a volcanic flow of tears, an eruption I was unable to contain. One of the resident nuns kindly guided me to her living quarters, where I spent the rest of the day, my unending tears the only thing keeping me company in that solitary space. I mourned the loss of my brother. I longed for him.

Four years later, in the spring of 1996, Uncle Derry, the one person in my life whose love has been a constant, from my arrival in the Currie family to the present, told me that Rob had contacted him. Rob had read in the newspaper that a man named John Currie had died and thought that might have been our other uncle. It wasn't. It came as no surprise that Uncle Derry was the person Rob contacted to find out; he was a safe haven, and Rob knew that in reaching out to him, he would be received with unconditional love and kindness.

I was over the moon just to know he was alive and doing okay. I asked Uncle Derry to ask for Rob's permission to give me his number. That was how I reconnected with my little brother. During long-distance calls from Halifax to Winnipeg, we made plans to spend some time together when I came for a visit that summer. We wanted to meet somewhere his whole family could come, where Rob's young kids could have fun, and we could catch up. We needed a place where we could both feel comfortable, where we could relax and let the intensity of our reunion disperse. We tried to think of a place where we all of us would have the different kinds of space we needed. When Uncle Derry and Aunt Charlene offered to host us at the cottage, we accepted without hesitation.

So it was at Netley Creek that Rob arrived in my life for the second time.

I sat on the dock, dangling my feet in the cool water, waiting for my brother. To say I was excited would be an understatement. Only the water—part of the river system that has been there for me throughout my whole life—could dilute the potent emotional cocktail that coursed through me.

The cottage's driveway is around back, so the first indication I had of their arrival was the sound of car doors closing. Seconds later, my grateful eyes drank in the sight of Rob coming around the corner of the cottage, my three-year-old nephew in his burly arms, closely followed by my five-year-old niece and my sister-in-law. Rob placed his little son down on the ground beside him. I ran across the grass and launched myself into a huge hug, enfolded in the arms of the person who knew me and the truth of my experience better than anyone else on the planet.

"Hey, sis." Until I met my birth siblings, I had only ever heard this greeting from Rob. That one little syllable, *sis*, washed away years of loneliness.

"Oh my god, Rob, it's *so* good to see you!" He pretty much squeezed the words out of me.

I squatted to greet my niece, eye to eye. "Hi, there. It's good to meet you." I had met her once when she was a year old but knew she couldn't remember that. It was when Rob and his family had come back to Uncle Derry's house after our grandmother's funeral. So heavy was the weight of shame on Rob, created by our adoptive mother's revisionist lies about him and his disappearance told to all our relatives, that he had not felt safe at the family gathering. His family had not ventured any farther than the kitchen and stayed only for minutes. Just as well my niece didn't remember that.

Rob and I took the kids over to the tire swing. We said nothing about our years without contact—the kids were the measure of that. All that hurt and misunderstanding was neutralized by the powerful goodness of being together again. Our conversation skipped like a stone across descriptions of our current lives, the underlying story of our growing-up years carried wordlessly between us, a big trunk of troubles. Our hands slid easily into the well-worn handles. We could carry this together while doing other things; we always had.

The lake, our nickname for our spot on the creek, was the perfect place to be. We sat in the sun on lawn chairs, savouring each other's presence along with cold drinks and snacks. My nephew's resemblance to his dad when Rob was that age was startling, and my niece looked a lot like her mom. I took my time getting to know the kids, just hanging out by the water, playing and swimming. Of course, we had to go out in the boat. Uncle Derry steered us through the reedy channels deep into the marsh, to all the spots Rob and I remembered from our childhood fishing expeditions. Our boat ride took us very close to the East Channel, where the army John A. MacDonald had mustered to put down Louis Riel's provisional government had paddled in ominous silence in the fall of 1870 on their way to lay siege to Upper Fort Garry. Fast-forward two years from that day, and I would know that Rob and I were cruising through the traditional territory of our ancestors, the *maskîkwa*, but on that boat ride, we were returning to a more recent history. When I look at the many photos I took to try to capture that extraordinary day, the ones of Rob in the boat, flanked by his children in their chunky life jackets, everyone grinning ear to ear, are the happiest I ever saw him.

In November of that year, I sent Rob a birthday gift in the mail. I'd asked him on one of our frequent calls to wait until I could be on the phone with him to open it. One of the photographs I had taken on the day of our reunion at Netley was of his two children, my nephew sitting on the small beach and my niece standing in the water not far from her little brother. When I first saw the photo, I was struck by its similarity to one of Rob and me around the same age, sitting next to each other on the grass just a few feet from where his children would play more than thirty years later. I brought both photographs to the camera shop and asked if they could make a print of the recent photo in black and white to match the one taken in the early sixties and frame them together, side by side. When I picked up Rob's gift from the shop, the man who waited on me could not believe that the two little boys were not the same person.

There was a bit of a kerfuffle on the receiving end; nobody had been home when the courier arrived, and the parcel had been left with the neighbours. But once Rob had it, he called me as per my request, and I could hear the brown paper tearing as he opened it. Then he wasn't there, and my sister-in-law came on the phone.

"Um, he's kind of emotional right now," she said. "Give him a minute."

I would have given Rob the world. All I had given him was a picture of the two of us sitting on the ground, sharing a box of animal crackers, and a picture of his own children in almost the exact same spot, his son the spitting image of Rob as a toddler. The simple act of noticing that in a life so fragmented by disruption and disconnection, there was some continuity.

Scent of pine needles and sea salt on the cool autumn breeze, the smell of Salt Spring Island. I was the antithesis of the fall air that was so light, warm, and fragrant as I walked, head down, along the side of the road toward Ganges. Heavy with despair. Worn down to the point of being less than threadbare. Completely exposed in a place that had never been safe. I knew I had to leave.

Whenever I visited my adoptive parents, I never stayed longer than a few days. Since it was too far and too expensive a trip to make for a short time, I always tried to tack a visit with them on to something else. I don't recall what other reason I had to be in BC that time, in the fall of 1997. I had arrived on the island by the afternoon ferry. I'd deposited my bags in their den, which doubled as a guest room thanks to a comfy Hide-A-Bed, and joined my parents in the living room for a drink before dinner, as was their custom. There were usually a few hours of simple pleasure in seeing each other after a year or two before the tired old tension came roaring back. But this time, we didn't last that long.

I had reconnected with Rob that summer. Our mother was no doubt anxious about that, as Rob's reappearance might wreak havoc with the revisionist history she'd constructed to explain what had happened with him. In her version, she was the victim: the poor loving, long-suffering mother who martyred herself on the cross of heroic parenting for a lost cause of a son too damaged to fix before she'd even met him. She presented as curious on that lovely autumn afternoon, as if she merely wanted to know how he was—but what she really wanted was to shore up her story and make sure his presence did not disrupt her fabricated narrative. I had anticipated this and already resolved not to discuss Rob with them at all. What I had not anticipated was how relentless my mother would be.

She tried to snare me into talking about him by asking me why I thought he'd made himself scarce for so long. I tried three times to deflect her question and redirect us into safer territory. "I'm not sure we really want to talk about this, Mom." "I'd rather talk about how you two are doing. Did you get out on the boat much this summer?" And, finally, "Mom, I just don't think this is a good idea." I felt like Saint Peter on the day of the crucifixion. Three times he denied Christ, and three times I denied my mother's request to engage in the conversation she was determined to have.

Then she cried. I was surprised; she didn't use that weapon very often. She had turned the tide against me; if I didn't agree to talk about this in the face of her tears, then *I* was being cruel to *her*. She was a master manipulator.

I told my parents that I could not speak for Rob, only my own experience, and that some of my feelings were shared by him. That was the best I could offer in terms of shedding any light on the subject.

I had long since learned that, for those of us healing from childhood abuse, confronting one's abusers is not necessary for healing to happen. For some, confronting one's abusers can be an important and empowering part of the process, particularly when the perpetrators are willing and able to take responsibility for the harm they caused when the violation happened and in its aftermath. For others though, including me, there is little to be gained from attempting an honest conversation with those who abused us, particularly when it's unlikely that our feelings will be validated and more likely to be a crazy-making encounter with someone who lives in a universe of their own design, where all their actions are reasonable and justified. I had made my peace with what they had done to me, so I could talk about that without feeling unsafe. I had not, however, made my peace with what they had done to my younger brother, so I would not venture out onto that thin ice.

I told them they might find what I had to say hard to hear and I wanted them to know that I bore them no ill will. That I had come to believe they had done the best they could.

Then I said it had taken me a long time to heal from being physically hit and hurt by them. (I knew better than to talk about the emotional abuse—understanding that was well and truly outside of their wheelhouse.) I clarified that although I believed corporal punishment was wrong—and the law backs me up on this now—it was not the many spankings that I was referring to. I was talking about being hit when Mom or Dad was out of control; this had terrified me as a child.

Mom looked at me with a blank look on her face. Dad was giving me his full attention. Mom asked me what I meant. I took a breath and continued, reminding her of the times she'd pulled my hair, punched me with closed fists, kicked me. She was speechless. I had crossed what she thought was an impermeable line from the acceptable family story into the truth.

Dad was shocked: "Your mother has never raised her fist to anyone!"

I took another breath, turning to face him.

"That's not true."

In the thousand-watt glare of that light bulb moment, I saw that Dad did not know. That she had not told him. That when he had once said to me, "I don't know what it is with you and your mother," he really hadn't known. That the line we three kids had always been fed that they were together on everything, a united front, wasn't true either. That my mother's abusive behaviour toward Rob and me was something she had kept from our father.

It was my turn to be shocked. I'd actually believed them when they said that as parents, they were always aware of what the other was doing. I shook my head in slow motion, rearranging my mother's lies into truth in my mind.

The air in the room rippled; time went sideways. I suddenly felt like I was in the house of mirrors at the Red River Ex, wobbling with vertigo, my feet not sure of the floor. Our shared space as a family was not used to truth. It shook all the niceties down, made it feel like the walls were collapsing. Because I had not grasped the depth and breadth of the deceit involved, I was not ready for the depth and breadth of disorientation the truth would bring. We were in some kind of *Twilight Zone* reality.

I said I needed to go for a walk.

Wearing my heavy black-leather biker jacket like armour, I walked, the beauty of the island blurred by my tears. Tears acknowledging that I had come to the end of a long road. Tears acknowledging that I no longer had a place in this family, a family that had been built on a twisted-up middle-class fantasy that I was no longer willing to play along with. Tears of relief.

I understand integrity to be when we are the same on the outside as we are on the inside. I shed tears of pride that I had brought some integrity into that space. Calm tears.

When I got back to their house, all the shades were drawn. Mom had taken to her bed, curtains drawn, door closed. Dad told me that she had a migraine, that she was very upset. I walked to the phone and called to find out when the next ferry would be leaving. Turned out I had to stay overnight and catch the ferry in the morning.

I went into the den and repacked the few things I had taken out of my suitcase, a cone of silence around me. I was protecting myself. *It's okay*, I thought, *I can do self-contained*. Dad and I were orbiting around each other in the poisoned air; he was also orbiting around her. Conversation was impossible. I decided to get into the hot tub.

At one point, while walking past me, he stopped long enough to say, "You really shouldn't have said that about your mother."

To which I replied, "If you'll recall, I tried to prevent this. Anyway, I'm leaving on the morning ferry. You know that's best."

"You have a ticket?"

"Yes."

"I'll drive you."

We spent the rest of the evening and the early part of the next morning in a no-contact improv dance. I was packed, waiting. Then Irene emerged from the bedroom. She wanted to talk. To reassert the myth of the normalcy of our family and relegate everything I had said back into silence.

She sat on the couch. I sat on the floor. I'm not sure why. Maybe to feel grounded. Because all I could do, all I had to do, was hold my seat. I had nothing more to say. There was nothing to be gained from having this conversation, because the only thing I could do that would make me marginally acceptable to her would be to recant, say I had been lying, or better yet, reassure her that I must have been really messed up in those first eight months of my life before I came to them and that was why I had lied. I was not going to do any of that, so it was just a matter of staying grounded while her toxic commentary flowed over me. I focused only on not letting it stick.

Standing on the outside deck once the ferry had left Long Harbour, there was no looking back, no last wave to my dad. I bathed in the medicine that is the beauty of the Gulf Islands. My spirit drank in peace from the islands and the ocean.

Something had shifted. It seemed clear in that moment that I would not be travelling this way again for a long time, if ever. But without a reason to come, I knew I wouldn't see the amazing beauty of this place as often, and that made me sad. I felt certain that I would never see my adoptive parents again, but that did not make me sad. It was impossible to be genuine with them, and I was no longer willing to perform as they required. They hadn't changed, but I had.

Knowing I could sit with and deflect an assault on my spirit, stay true to myself, walk away—that changed me. Even more important, knowing that I could choose not to spend time with people who hurt my spirit recalibrated my inner compass.

The freeing up of my heart in those twenty-four hours made it possible for me to respond to them both with love and support when my dad was diagnosed with a terminal illness the following spring.

# MY FIRST CLIENT

Back in Mi'kma'ki, I was working on getting my master's degree in counselling and had to find a practicum placement. I wanted to be mentored by a mental health professional who had an awareness of spirituality. I knew therapy was about healing and that there is a connection between the two; I was aware of my own spirit and the part it played in my resilience. I understood that this would never be something I would impose in any way on the people I worked with; I just wanted to learn from a therapist who acknowledged a spiritual aspect to our lives and had a holistic approach to their practice.

This was another manifestation of blood memory guiding my life choices. Having yet to reconnect with my family and culture, I did not consciously know that in the Anishinaabe world view and concepts of health and healing, well-being is understood as a dynamic balance between the mental, emotional, physical, and spiritual aspects of our being.

I was still recovering from an upbringing steeped in the rancid contradictions, pervasive sexism, and rampant abuse within the Catholic Church, so I wasn't looking for anyone to tell me what to believe, what to think, or how to live my life. I understood the value of having a community of people with whom to share spiritual practice, and I had started attending services at the Universalist Unitarian Church in Halifax. In my experience, the Unitarian community was a motley crew of people who did not ascribe to any particular belief system but respected all the wisdom traditions from around the world, the only shared belief being that everyone is on their own quest for meaning. Some of the people I met there were kindred souls and became lifelong friends; some I would never have crossed paths with anywhere else. A bunch of questers and questioners—perfect for me.

I approached a woman in that community who was a therapist and asked her if it might be possible to do my placement with her. I did not have a checklist of the qualities I was looking for; I was sensing my way to the right teacher for me. I knew I did not want to learn from someone wedded to the mainstream medical model of mental health care who saw people through the lens of the DSM-5 (the *Diagnostic and Statistical Manual of Mental Health Disorders, Fifth Edition,* a compendium of symptoms, disorders, and criteria used by psychiatrists and other mainstream mental health practitioners to diagnose). I did not want to approach my work by looking for what was wrong with people. I wanted a teacher who was integrated within themselves, with heart and spirit in the mix, freed from the dominance of rational cognition as the only or best way of knowing. From her choice to be part of the Unitarian community, her contributions to open discussions in the services I went to, and just from her presence, I thought this therapist would be a good person to learn from. I was delighted when she agreed to take me on. I entered into a rich learning experience replete with opportunities, risk-taking, support, exemplary compassion, and deep wisdom. It turned out that this woman, who became my supervisor and main teacher, was regarded by many in the field as one of the best therapists working in Nova Scotia at the time. The director of my counselling program was amazed at my good fortune.

The first client I worked with on my own was "Kate," a fifteen-year-old young woman with an intensely belligerent attitude and zero interest in coming to counselling. Now, having worked as a therapist for almost thirty years, I can honestly say she was the toughest client I have ever had. At the time, I did not appreciate the challenge or feel up to it, but now I am grateful that I cut my teeth on building a therapeutic relationship that taught me so much and gave me the confidence to face whomever and whatever might come my way in the years that followed.

There had been a lot of conflict between Kate and her parents, and she was living in a group home at the time. She was the adopted daughter of a couple who also had a biological child, Kate's younger sister. The parents were in therapy with my supervisor, I was working with Kate, and there was the option of doing family therapy, with all of us participating.

With Kate and her family's permission, my teacher sometimes observed my sessions with her through a two-way mirror, listening to us through a microphone suspended from the ceiling and giving me occasional suggestions through an earbud I wore. It was like the voice of God speaking in my head. With this expert guidance, I found my way to connecting with Kate. I recall one session early on, when we were sitting across from each other, my teacher behind the mirror and Kate slumped so far down in her chair that she was about to slide onto the floor. I, the green and eager therapist, was leaning in, exuding the positive energy I naively thought she would find irresistible. Nodding is a gesture taught as part of active listening. When I viewed the video of that session—recording sessions was a required part of my master's program, and Kate and her parents had agreed to this—I was dismayed to see my head nodding so frequently that I looked like a bobblehead ornament on somebody's dashboard. I toned down the nodding after that.

My teacher knew a better approach and, through the earbud, instructed me to slump down in my chair as well. I did. Then she told me to slowly and gradually shift to sitting upright in my seat. I did. Miraculously, Kate slowly sat up in her chair too! That was my first lesson in movement synchrony, which is based on the knowledge that we have a cluster of neurons that are designed to mirror another person's body language; mirroring is a way we can express and experience empathy through our bodies. Kate and I began to feel connected that day. We worked together for the better part of a year, the sessions becoming more and more enjoyable as our working partnership grew stronger. Kate moved back in with her family. She kept in touch with me for several years after leaving home and establishing herself in her adult life in another part of the province.

Besides learning counselling skills in my work with Kate, I also had to learn to recognize and dispel intrusive thoughts, because this family's situation echoed Rob's experience in our adoptive family in many ways. Her parents had a hard time relating to her, as her personality was unlike anyone else's in the family, and she did not feel she belonged. She was acting out, and her parents did not know what to do. All of this was just like Rob's experience. But there were also clear differences between their family and ours. When Kate's behaviour reached a point where her parents felt they did not have the resources to cope and Kate went to live in a group home, her parents sought help for themselves and for her separately. They visited her on a regular basis, took her on outings, and she came home for visits. She was still included in their family rituals on special occasions; they would pick her up and bring her home so she could participate. She was still part of the family.

Her parents did not abandon her. They did not see adoption as coming with a return policy. And their relationships healed over time. They got through those rough years and stayed connected as family in ways that strengthened their sense of belonging with each other.

I would go home in the evenings on the days I had worked with Kate, reflecting on all of this in light of having lost my brother when our parents sent him away. It was healing for me to witness parents making another choice, their love for their child truly unconditional, their egos put aside so they could honour the commitment inherent in being a parent, regardless of the way that sacred responsibility comes. I felt connected with this family, my spirit responding to the sturdy love, deep respect, and quiet, steady courage of these parents. In the midst of the pain they were feeling, each member of the family was willing to learn about and accept the truth of who each other really was. They were honest in their communication, humble enough to reach out for help, accept suggestions, and try new ways of being with each other. They were wise in letting the healing take the time it took, which in this case was a couple of years.

Later, with the help of Elders from my Métis homeland and Mi'kma'ki, I came to understand the power of the Seven Sacred Teachings and embrace their wisdom as a path to healing. Referred to as the Seven Grandfather Teachings in Anishinaabe culture, they are considered to be foundational to living a good life. There are several versions of the teachings and their origins among different Indigenous nations; all are based on the belief that the teachings were given to the people by Creator to guide us. The seven teachings are LOVE, RESPECT, COURAGE, TRUTH, HONESTY, HUMILITY, and WISDOM.

# LETTERS

I sat in the windowless computer lab at Acadia University, leaning into the screen as if proximity could help me solve its mysteries. The rest of my counselling class was there too. It was the midnineties, and most of us were not yet adept at using the internet; this tutorial was compulsory. We had been instructed to choose a topic that interested us and look up information about it on the web. I forget what I typed in—technical knowledge never stays with me very long, pushed off the loading dock of my memory by all the other things I care so much more about. One online bulletin board took me to an alphabetical list of topics, which I scrolled through until I landed on "Adoption." I slowed my scrolling. This might be interesting. A little farther down, I saw "Adoption—Manitoba" and clicked on that.

What I read on that site transported me instantly: I was back in Winnipeg, where, the website explained, adult adoptees could now apply to have an active search to find our birth mothers. This was life-changing news. The last time I had checked, non-identifying information from my file was all that was available. I stumbled through the rest of the day in a fog.

Research in the area of social work and social policy suggests that a shift in thinking about adoption took place during the 1980s and 1990s. In the eighties, if an adult adoptee wanted to find out more about where they came from, all that was available was non-identifying information and registration on an agency-administered post-adoption registry. Upon receiving a written request, the adoptee's file would be reviewed, and non-identifying information such as the mother's physical characteristics, health information, education, and occupation would be sent to them. I had requested and received some information in 1985, actually more than would usually be the case, because my mother had filled out an optional questionnaire called a social history. She had wanted me to know some things. Descriptions of her and her mother, enough details to know I was like them. The good feeling from those few typewritten pages lasted ten years. I chose not to put my name on the post-adoption registry, which was a record of adoptees and birth family members interested in having contact with each other. If the person who was adopted and someone from their birth family both voluntarily registered, they would be put in touch with each other. At that time, no action was taken to let the other party know that their relative was interested in connecting with them. Like many adoptees, I had not placed my name on the post-adoption registry because I knew that if I heard nothing, that would mean that nobody in my birth family was interested in having contact with me, and I was afraid of how I might feel if that were the case.

The history of adoption is circular. Prior to the 1930s, most cultural communities had informal kinship adoptions, agreements made within extended families when a baby was born who could not be cared for by their mother. Many communities, notably Indigenous and Black communities here in Canada, continued these practices even after provincial legislation created agencies that took over adoption arrangements.

The first child welfare agency in Canada was established in the 1890s in Ontario to respond to child labour, homelessness, and juvenile delinquency. There can be no doubt that there were children who needed help. The Canadian government contributed to creating this need by bringing in over one hundred thousand children from the United Kingdom between 1869 and 1932, usually from very poor families, in a juvenile immigration program designed to supply Canadian farmers with cheap labour. Placing these children was part of the impetus for the development of the child welfare system.

By the 1930s, adoption programs administered by provincial agencies were being rolled out. Shame and secrecy surrounded adoption, peaking in the 1950s, when the ideal of the nuclear family gained ascendancy, pressuring women to live up to harsh and limiting standards of supposedly "proper" behaviour. This secrecy was rooted in patriarchal notions of women and children as property. Those of us born out of wedlock, which constituted the majority of children "given up" for adoption, were considered an affront to men's social control of women. The unmarried women whose hookups with nameless and blameless men resulted in our being born were perceived as bringing shame upon their families—read: fathers—whose lack of control over their property could cost them leverage in the ongoing pursuit of power and privilege. Secrecy surrounding adoption was intended to protect the reputations of these men and "their" families, in which the unwed mothers and their babies had to be hidden until a home could be found for the child and the mother could return to the family and be put back on the marriage market, restoring the status of the family in "decent" society. Hence the quiet whisking away of these women to homes for unwed mothers, as well as the lies made up by their families to explain their absence.

The secrecy was also intended to protect the privacy of the couples who adopted these unwanted children. Nobody needed to know, the thinking went, and once the children were placed, it was thought that where we came from was best forgotten by everyone. Adopted children were expected to act as if we were born into the adoptive families we ended up in.

The Sixties Scoop added another layer of pain and loss: the cultural genocide of reducing Indigenous populations by forcing us to leave behind our Indigenous identities and communities, combined with the assimilationist practice of transplanting us in unfamiliar ground where we would be taught the social norms of whiteness, which according to the prevailing "wisdom" of the time was seen as a step up for us.

Adopted children were seen as not equal to biological children. My adoptive mother told me that when she and my dad decided to adopt, they were cautioned against it by several of their friends, who said things like, "You don't know what you're getting." Note how this language reflects the values of the dominant culture, which regarded children as property. She also told me more than once, in moments of conflict between us, that if she had to make the choice all over again, she would still adopt me. I gathered that I was to feel grateful for her long-suffering charity.

Overall, *adoption* was considered somewhat indelicate, a word that had an unpleasant aftertaste, necessary but unfortunate. A settler individual once said to me that adoption always comes from tragedy. I thought of a Black family I know in which the child of the oldest daughter, conceived at a time when the young mother was doing post-secondary studies and trying to get a foothold in life on her own, was raised by the young mom's parents, becoming the youngest sibling in that family. That was a response to practical challenges, not a tragedy. Granted, there are babies born into tragic situations; some will become adoptees, and some will grow up in unsafe birth families. But the notion that adoption is always a result of a tragedy is based on a class-bias-riddled belief that the nuclear family model, i.e., married parents with children, is the only acceptable form of family. This way of thinking has more to do with reinforcing white privilege, patriarchal social control, and a class-based society than with supporting healthy family life. Who gets to define what constitutes a tragedy? Through what lens are we looking when we judge a circumstance as tragic? If people accept the notion that adopting a child is saving that child, the dominant narrative that adoption is always about helping stays intact.

Many cultural communities have more flexible beliefs about healthy ways to raise children. It is only recently that some of these kinship and community models of adoption are beginning to be recognized as valid by the dominant culture in its stubborn adherence to Eurocentric definitions of what constitutes family.

In recent years, attitudes and policy regarding adoption have circled back and returned to valuing open adoptions and kinship placements in the child's community of origin. The decades-long detour from that original wisdom damaged many people. In my case, having grown up with the silence and secrecy around where I came from, I internalized that I would never know who my people were, and with no other mindset available, I accepted that for many years.

Once I found out that requesting a search for my birth mother was possible, I made plans to proceed. The next time I went to Winnipeg, I made an appointment at Winnipeg Child and Family Services. I showed up in the depressing office painted institutional green and

crammed with too many desks, papers piled on every surface and over-
flowing from grey-metal filing cabinets. I paid the fee and filed the
application. My older adoptive brother had warned me that it could
take a long time; it had taken seven years for him to receive any information. Needless to say, I was not holding my breath.

I love kids. I've wanted to be a mother all my life, with the exception of
a brief period when I was twelve and made the decision never to have
children because my adoptive mother repeatedly told me that when I
became a mother, I would be just like her. The idea that I'd turn out the
same as her scared me. When I couldn't deny my deep longing to be
a mother someday, I started keeping a notebook. I wrote down all the
things she did that hurt me so when I had children of my own, I could
refer to this list and remember what not to do. After keeping that notebook hidden for a couple of years, I decided to destroy it, concerned
that if something ever happened to me and my mother found it, her
feelings would be hurt. I've never wanted to hurt my adoptive mother,
then or now. I just stay far enough away that she cannot hurt me.

Once I passed the watermark of my midthirties, I felt the need to
prepare myself for the possibility that I would not have a child of my
own. I had beautiful, committed relationships with other peoples' children whom I knew would be part of my life forever, and I knew I could
adopt, but accepting that I might never give birth to a child was an
emotional hurdle that was looming just ahead. I started to think about
how I would deal with that.

Then I had a clairaudient experience. I heard a voice. I can say for
certain that it was definitely not just a thought; the voice was distinct
from the silent feel of a thought. It was multilayered, like voices doubled
in a recording studio with a split second of delay so you can hear the
fullness. It had a resonant quality that commanded attention. The voice
said, "You are not going to have a child until you find your mother." I
was startled when I heard it, but unafraid. Accepting that this was a
one-way, one-time statement, not an opener for conversation, I considered its meaning. I was thirty-six. If it took Child and Family Services
as long to find my birth mother as had taken them to find my older
brother's, I would be in my early forties by that time. My biological

clock didn't like those odds. Still, I knew this message had come to me for a reason, and so I decided to stop thinking I might not ever get pregnant. Maybe the message was warning me away from making a significant shift in my hopes and plans, ensuring I would not focus on creating a life that excluded being a parent.

It took them less than a year to find my mother. I learned that when the adoptee is as old as I was, their file can jump the queue, in consideration of the likelihood that the birth mother is elderly and may not be around for much longer. The other thing that worked in my favour is that the first step in the search is to check the phone book, and my mother was listed.

In April of 1998, a letter arrived from the agency. My mother had been found and was interested in meeting me! The next step was for me to call the social worker who had written the letter so we could discuss the process.

Whenever I tell this story, I joke about how weird it was for me as a psychotherapist to be the client on that call, to be "social worked." I tell that story about the phone call because it's a feeling I can describe, while most of what I was feeling was beyond words. This is why it's so important for adoptees—Sixties Scoop survivors in my case—to get together so we can experience being understood without having to worry about explaining things beyond the reach of language.

It was on that phone call that I found out I am Métis. I had learned from the non-identifying information I had already received that my mother's first language was French. I am not fluently bilingual and was worried that my mother and I might not be able to communicate. I recall feeling anxious as I asked the social worker whether my mother spoke English. I heard papers rustling on the other end of the phone as she looked for the answer to my question. As she leafed through my file, she said absent-mindedly, "Hmm, let's see now ... I know that she's Métis ..."

"What?"

The moment swelled to many times its natural size so it could hold my heart.

*I am Métis.*

I could feel my spirit uncurling, unfurling, as if awakening from a long, deep sleep. It was all I could do to hold up my end of the conversation after that. My energy surged; I felt like I could run for miles. My spirit was stretching, expanding to fill the space that was opening in which I could finally be myself.

It was on me to write the first letter. This is because adoptees search for their birth parents for different reasons. Some want only their family medical history, some want to meet just once, some hope for an ongoing relationship. The person who requested the search is asked to tell their birth family member why they did so.

It took me over two months to write that letter. Why that long? After the excitement of finding her and knowing that she wanted to meet me, what was I waiting for?

Fear was part of it. While I had never fantasized about having another, much better family out there somewhere, as many unhappy adopted children do, I was not in a hurry to experience more pain from a family member. The happy, fulfilling life I had created for myself since leaving home almost twenty years earlier had taken a lot of courage and determination and made me very self-sufficient. The truth is that family, in the conventional sense, did not take up much space in my life and was not one of my priorities. I had spent a considerable amount of time and energy ensuring my life was full and calm. I wasn't sure how much disruption I was up for. For the rest of April, all of May, and the first part of June 1998, I just thought about writing the letter.

I went to my professional association's annual conference in Montreal that June. I have always found it easier to contemplate big life questions when I am away from home. One day, I skipped out of the conference and headed for Old Montreal. I found a café with an outdoor patio and, sitting in the warmth of the sun, wrote, "Dear Claudette."

Fear distorts. When we put off doing something because we are afraid of what might happen, the worst-case scenario that we imagine takes on monstrous proportions. Quite often, once we get around to doing the thing we're afraid of, we discover that it wasn't as hard as we thought it would be. Writing my first letter to Maman was like that. I thanked her for being willing to meet me, told her that I had never felt any ill will toward her and that I would like to meet her too. I let her know that I was very interested in learning more about my history and culture as a member of the Métis Nation and that I was open to an ongoing relationship.

I did not feel any worry while waiting for a reply. I had been invited to join the practice where I'd done my counselling practicum, and I was working there part-time. I thought about the letter I was waiting for now and then, but I wasn't sitting on the mailbox. I now know that I was unconsciously processing and preparing for the profound changes that had been initiated. The fact that Maman and I were communicating via snail mail provided time and space for this.

In an Origins Canada article[18] about factors that influence adoption reunion outcomes, both parties are advised to take their time. There is a lot to work through: new information, feelings, and all the questions that arise. And it's not like there was nothing else happening in my life in the time between writing to my birth mother and receiving her reply.

My birth mother was less hesitant about writing than I had been, and on a beautiful morning in early July, I opened the front door of my apartment and stepped into the vestibule, where the mail for me and my upstairs neighbour was stuffed through a slot in the outer door.

I spied an envelope with unfamiliar handwriting in the sheaf I picked up off the floor. A Winnipeg return address! My heart raced. I walked through my place to the stairs to my back door and out into the backyard and gardens I shared with other members of my housing co-op—a beautiful oasis in the North End of Halifax, where green space is not abundant. I had to have my feet on the earth to read this letter.

Seated at the picnic table, surrounded by colourful perennials and vegetable gardens, I opened it. Maman, as I came to call her—*Mom* reminded me too much of my adoptive mother—had sent a card and a separate written letter. As I opened the folded letter, two photos fell out.

There she was.

Maman was an attractive woman. She was in her midsixties in the photographs, taken on the occasion of her retirement from the renal dialysis unit at the Winnipeg Health Sciences Centre, where she worked as a receptionist for many years. One of them was taken in a restaurant with some friends from work when they were out celebrating this milestone. The other—the one that pierced me deeply—was of her sitting at her desk on the unit. I recognized myself in her. Not just her eyes and her smile, but the way she was sitting, the way she inhabited herself. I felt drawn right into her. The way her arm was resting on her lap—I could feel it in my own body. *That's the way I hold my arm, the way I carry myself*, I thought, tears spilling from my eyes. I could have been looking at a photograph of myself in thirty years' time.

She was a part of me. I was a part of her.

And I looked like her.

For an individual who has never been told that they look like someone in their family, who has always felt different from everyone around them, this moment of realization is profound. Until that moment, I'd had no idea what it felt like to have that visible connection with someone, and a feeling of belonging rose up in me from somewhere so deep I hadn't even known it was there.

Her letter was open and loving and respectful; she expressed awareness that this experience might be overwhelming for me, and she wanted me to move through it at my own pace. She told me about my eight older brothers and sisters and that two of my sisters had died in accidents—one in a car, one on a motorcycle. My joy was tainted by grief: I would never be able to meet them. She gave me her phone number and invited me to call her whenever I was ready.

Synchronicity is a bright thread in the tapestry of my life, strong enough to weave many disparate parts together. My mother's letter arrived a half-hour before I was going to have lunch with two of my dearest friends, Muriel Duckworth and Betty Peterson. Anyone who was involved in social justice activism in Nova Scotia from the 1960s through to the first decade of this millennium knows of these extraordinary women. Their leadership and tireless efforts in the Nova Scotia chapter of the Canadian Voice of Women for Peace is perhaps what they are best known for, but their compassion and commitment to solidarity was also expressed in many other issues: working to eliminate racism; marching for equality for women; mobilizing for justice for Indigenous Peoples; advocating for queer rights, fair labour practices, affordable housing, and an end to poverty. In addition to teaching me so much about transformative social change, both of them nurtured me, two of the dozen or so amazing older women in my life who have mothered me.

There was no better place for me to go right after receiving my first ever letter from my birth mother than to have lunch with the two of them at Muriel's place, a plan we had made weeks prior.

I don't remember driving down Agricola to Young Street or going up the elevator in the Bayers Park Apartments, but I do recall knocking on the door with my heart knocking just as loudly in my chest. Betty opened the door, having arrived just ahead of me from her suite a couple of floors down. As soon as I saw her, I burst into tears.

"Look! Look what came in the mail today!" I waved the letter in front of her, everything blurry as she took my arm and guided me into the living room. I hugged and kissed them both, and when we were seated, I read the letter from Maman out loud. They cried with me.

I can still see their faces gazing at me with such love and understanding, holding me steady as love, regret, relief, grief, and hope flooded every cell in my being. They are gone now, each having lived to be one hundred. Four the Moment, an a cappella quartet I was a member of for many years along with three African Nova Scotian women, sang at both of their hundredth birthday parties. When I greeted Betty at her party, all she could talk about was how she had never forgotten that amazing day and the letter.

I had the honour of drumming and singing the Cree Travelling Song for each of them when they crossed over to Spirit. By then I had met my oldest sister, who made sure I learned some of the traditional drum songs from our territory. When we drum, we are connecting to the heartbeat of Mother Earth and to all our mothers, whose heartbeat is the first sound we hear.

I did not have my birth mother in my life for my first thirty-eight years, and the mother I lived with for my first seventeen was not able to love me in a healthy, nurturing way. But I have had many mothers, and they have been there for the most important moments of my life.

I met my birth mother in July of 1998. I was pregnant by December of that year. Maman came to Halifax to be there when my baby was born. My link to my people had been broken but was repaired in time for my son: he has never had to live one minute without knowing who he is.

# THE MOMENT

words
like seeds

scatter on the page

meaning
blooms

I
know now
why I am this way

Métis
girl

# THE PHONE CALL

When I received my Spirit Name, Green Turtle Woman, it was clear to everyone who knew me just how appropriate it was. In all important matters, I move slowly. I dwell close to the earth, going forward steadily, step by careful step.

In the twenty years since I left my adoptive home, "family" in the conventional sense had receded into the periphery of my life. My dad had crossed over the previous winter; I had made a couple of trips to Salt Spring during the course of his illness and was there when he died. According to his wishes, I sang at his funeral. After his death, I maintained occasional contact with my adoptive mother and older brother. I was in touch with Rob on a regular basis, but other than that, family was a small part of my life. I had no sense of there being a void where family should have been. What I *was* missing was still outside the reach of my awareness: a deep knowledge of who I was, a sense of continuity with my ancestors, and a strong connection to my homeland.

I was curious about my birth mother and family, but I was not motivated by any feeling that I really needed them. Though I had recently—finally—experienced the simple comfort of knowing I was like some other people on the planet, I didn't know that I was missing anything. Not yet.

To the best of my knowledge, I was doing okay on my own. More than okay.

Wasn't I?

So, I didn't call her right away. Several days later, on a rare free evening, I picked up the phone and entered the phone number she had sent me.

Her voice on the other end of the line was warm and caring, enthusiastic yet calm. I recall excitement seeping through my protective go-to stance of caution. Conversation came easily despite the surreal backdrop: I was speaking with my mother for the first time, at the age of thirty-seven. We chatted about everyday things for a bit. Then she told me there was so much she wanted to tell me about our family, but she did not want to overwhelm me. I asked her to tell me whatever she wanted to share at that time.

First, she told me about her mother, my grandmother, Marie Thérèse Goulet Courchaine, a writer who went by the pen name Manie-Tobie. My grandmother was an extraordinary woman who lived a life ahead of her time by at least a couple of generations. She distinguished herself in school, winning a prize for the highest marks in French in the entire province. Though she married Joseph (Joe) Courchaine, who worked in road and bridge construction and was also a market gardener, she had her own career as a teacher. Her kids boarded at the local convent school in their hometown of St. Adolphe, and she taught in different places throughout the province, including day schools on First Nations reserves, to help bring money into the household during the Depression years. Although she and my grandfather lived apart some of the time, they had an amicable marriage. She was also a radio broadcaster, a singer-songwriter, a journalist, and a poet.

She wrote a regular column that appeared in numerous French and English newspapers throughout southern Manitoba. When she began to lose her eyesight in 1960 due to severe diabetes, she continued to write using a Braille typewriter. Her poetry won literary prizes, including one in France.

I was enthralled. Could my love of words, of reading and writing, be inherited from her?

Maman went on. Marie Thérèse's grandfather, Elzéar Goulet, had been a very close collaborator of Louis Riel's, holding the position of second-in-command of the Métis militia in Riel's provisional government in 1869 and 1870. A strong leader in the thriving Métis community at the Red River Settlement, Elzéar dedicated his life to the protection of our people and our traditional ways. He gave his life for our Nation, murdered in September 1870 by off-duty soldiers from the Wolseley expedition, which had been sent by John A. Macdonald to suppress the Métis resistance and clear the way for his plan to annex our homeland.

I felt such pride as I listened to my great-great-grandfather's story. I also felt deep sorrow, the depth and breadth of my loss coming into focus as I listened, my long-held solidarity with Indigenous struggles for sovereignty and self-determination coming home in my heart and making sense to me in a new way as I grieved for my family member whose life was brutally cut short because he stood up for our people.

I had bought a copy of Maggie Siggins's biography of Louis Riel[19] as soon as I learned I was Métis. I had not learned much about our history while growing up in the white suburbs of Winnipeg, and I had to catch up. When I hung up after talking with Maman, with promises to call again soon, I looked for Elzéar's name in the index at the back of Siggins's book. There it was, with several page references. Siggins wrote that Riel was very fond of Elzéar and was distressed when he heard about his death.

I carried that thick volume around with me everywhere for weeks, running my fingers over it each time I reached for something in my backpack as if it were my great-great-grandfather himself I was touching. I could not tear myself away from him. The only people who understood what I was feeling at that time were my sisters in Four the Moment. One of them told me that she'd had similar feelings when she read the narratives of people who had been enslaved: this is not just history, this is *family.*

Suddenly, I remembered a book that a Québécoise friend had given me after I had shared with her that my birth mother's first language was French. It was an anthology of Franco-Manitoban poetry.[20] I found myself wondering if maybe my grandmother was included in that collection. I took the book down from its place on my bookshelf, where it had been waiting for me to sit down with a French–English dictionary and explore its pages.

There she was. She looked up at me from a full-page black-and-white photograph. In her, I saw my mother and yes, myself, even down to the way she tilted her head for the picture. There was a biographical essay about her, a selection of her poems, and an academic article comparing her writing to the work of two other Franco-Manitoban poets. My friend had written an inscription in the front of the book. I turned to it and read, "*Voici une livre pour t'aider retrouver tes racines.*" Here is a book to help you find your roots.

Grandma had been with me, waiting for four years on my bookshelf for me to find her.

In the days following that first phone call with Maman, I wrote a song called "Trickster Time."

Eagle circles overhead, it's turning out just like she said
Hawk and raven don't mislead, you have exactly what you need
Picture in a book of poems, she came to me to guide me home
Four years later with my kin, catching up on how we've been

It's a time of magic
It's a time of magic

It's a gift of countless good to be finally understood
To know whose steps I'm walking in and what my family's history's been
Great-grandfather was stoned to death, in the river he found his rest
That river runs through everything I love, I work, I pray, I sing

It's a time of magic
It's a time of magic
Trickster time of magic

●–●–●

Things moved more quickly after the phone call. Within days, I had booked a flight to Winnipeg for later that month.

# THE DAY I MET MY MOTHER

I prepared myself for meeting my birth family by reading up on adoption reunion. One of the most important pieces of advice is to approach the reunion in a way that enables both parties to take their time. I learned about this and other factors that influence adoption reunion outcomes on the Origins Canada website:

- the readiness of the parties involved
- their life circumstances at the time of the reunion
- their age
- the attitudes and reactions of others
- their understanding of the past
- their motivation in wanting to reunite
- their expectations[21]

In my case, it was evident that both Maman and I were ready. Her life at that time was stable. She had positive relationships with some of her children and grandchildren, her ex-partner was living in their townhouse as a roommate and was still part of the family, and she had a close relationship with her sister, my auntie Pat. She had made her peace with her lack of contact with some of my siblings. As I would soon learn, my birth mother did what many people do: she blocked out unpleasant memories, especially those in which she had behaved badly, and even more especially those in which her behaviour had caused harm to her children. She'd made a firm decision to leave her past transgressions in the past. With the currency of selective memory, she had bought a form of happiness for herself.

As for me, I had realized a dream I'd had for many years and set out on what has become my life path: to help Indigenous people and communities heal through my work as a psychotherapist, community wellness worker, and writer. My life was going well.

We were both old enough to have let go of romantic notions of what our reunion could be. There was no denying the thirty-eight years that had passed since she walked away from me in the hospital—thirty-eight years full of more life experiences for both of us than we would ever be able to share. There was going to be a limit to how well we would ever know each other. We were both aware of this.

Maman had some explaining to do to my siblings; my existence had been kept a secret. Apparently, when the youngest of my brothers heard about me, he laughed and teased her: "So, Mom, are there any other brothers and sisters we don't know about?" Auntie Pat had known but kept the secret.

Meanwhile, in my adoptive family, I was only really close to Rob, Uncle Derry, and Aunt Charlene. Those three were happy for me and supportive. My older adoptive brother understood my curiosity, as he had made inquiries about his own birth mother. Back then, we didn't talk often, though we've since become closer. When I found out I was Métis, my adoptive mother had said she was happy for me. Now, however, she was unable to get her head and heart around the fact that I would have birth family members in my life, so there was never any conversation about this during our occasional long-distance phone calls. This did not upset me because my relationship with her had always been distant.

In terms of how the people we were close to felt, Maman and I were good to go.

We were both hopeful that we would stay connected and develop some kind of ongoing relationship, and we both knew that we had no way of knowing at the outset what that would look like. We were aligned in our openness and curiosity.

My deepest hope was that I would be able to connect with my cultural community. I wanted Maman's help with that, and although I didn't know for sure, I had a pretty good idea that her assistance would be forthcoming. She had already sent me a large box full of photos and information about my extended family, my ancestors, and current initiatives underway in the Manitoba Métis Federation, which she was involved in as a member of the Elders Local.

Charlene put down her mug of coffee on the white linen cloth of the dining room table.

"Don't you think it's time to go, Andrea?"

I had arrived in Winnipeg the evening before, and as usual on my visits home, I was staying with my Uncle Derry and Aunt Charlene. I've lost count of how many times I have descended that long escalator in the Winnipeg airport, scanning the arrivals area below and searching among the faces of those waiting there to find my uncle's welcoming smile. Now when I fly into Winnipeg, it's just as likely to be one of my biological brothers whose faces I am looking for, but on that trip it was still my uncle who was my anchor in the city that had become an unpredictable ocean of possibilities.

I had come to meet my birth mother and family.

Although Uncle Derry had retired by then from his position as Dean of Arts at the University of Manitoba, he was still involved in the social sciences research that had been his passion for decades, and he had a meeting on the day I was going to meet my mother. Aunt Charlene was going to drive me to her house. Uncle Derry, Aunt Charlene, and I had spent some time catching up the night before, and we continued to do so over breakfast, but I was stalling, and Charlene called me on it. It was time to go.

Knowing that my birth mother and I ticked all the boxes indicating the likelihood of a positive reunion experience did not make it easier to set off that morning. What was keeping me glued to my seat at the breakfast table? I had no rational reason to be afraid.

The answer to that question lies somewhere in the furthest reaches of my subconscious.

In her book *The Primal Wound: Understanding the Adopted Child*, Nancy Newton Verrier calls the wound left in the psyche of a child separated from their birth mother "primal." The word *primal* means "relating to an early stage of evolutionary development, primeval," "essential, fundamental."[22] Pre-consciousness. The mother whose womb we grow in is the first person with whom we have a relationship. The severing of that relationship is a traumatic experience for a newborn baby.

Everything we know about trauma has led us to understand that it is recorded in our bodies, our brains, our nervous systems, and, according to the teachings of my Métis, Anishinaabe, and Mi'kmaw Elders, in our spirits. Until childhood trauma is resolved, there is a part of us that stays the age we were when the trauma occurred. So it didn't matter that my thirty-eight-year-old self felt ready to meet my mother. The tiny baby who was abandoned at birth and whom I still carry inside me at the core of who I am was not. She was terrified. This whole plan did not feel safe to her.

I was a newly minted therapist, and I still had a lot to learn about trauma. The clarity with which I now see what was going on in that moment has come through years of training, being in therapy myself, and helping others heal from trauma.

The little one who had been abandoned all those years before was literally petrified. That early trauma had been triggered, and no matter how much my "wise adult" and rational mind told me it was okay to get up from the table and get into the car, it was really, really hard to move my body off that chair.

But I did it.

Claudette lived on the western edge of Winnipeg's North End—on the outskirts of the Indigenous community in the inner city—in a cluster of townhouses with a green space in the middle. Vehicle access was through a back lane.

Aunt Charlene eased the car slowly down the narrow lane, past all the postage-stamp backyards, until we came to the one we were looking for. A quick thank you and goodbye kiss to my aunt, and then I opened the car door and walked up the cement steps. Maman was on the other side of the screen door, where she had been watching for me.

She opened the door. Words of greeting light as feathers, smiles, a big hug, tears. She guided me through the kitchen into the living room, where I seated myself on a velvety-blue couch.

Maman had a beautiful smile, warm eyes, a soft voice. She asked me how my trip had been and was I tired, had I had any trouble finding the place. Behind the thin veil of small talk, we drank each other in. She pointed out all the art on the walls, original works by two of my sisters and one of my brothers. There was a lot of artistic talent in our family, and she was proud of each of her children.

Above the couch where I sat was a frame. Inside was a matte backing with several cut-outs where different photos could be placed. In the centre was a picture of Maman, with a photo of each of my eight siblings in the other oval holes. At the bottom, wedged between the frame and the matte, was the picture of me that I had sent her in my second letter. A space made for me in the family circle.

Over the course of this day that became its own time zone, I met several other family members. First, Maman's ex-boyfriend emerged from his room, where he had retreated to give us privacy for our initial meeting. He was a sweet, comical Caribbean man who insisted on referring to himself as my father. Although I never called him Dad, I interpreted this as his way of welcoming me. Then an exuberant nine-year-old boy burst through the back door and ran into the living room, thrusting a huge bouquet of flowers out in front of him before wrapping his arms around me and hugging me tight. This beautiful smiling face belonged to my cousin's son, and he was followed into the room by my aunt Pat, also eager to meet her long-lost grandniece but not as quick on her feet as her grandson.

The discussion of resemblances began right away. I looked like one of my sisters who had passed away too young, may she rest in power. But I also looked like another sister who lived in Ontario.

"There's no doubt she's one of yours, Claudie," Auntie Pat joked before turning to me. "Yup, you're definitely one of us."

The intensity lightened for a bit as the two sisters talked about different things. I had a moment to be an observer, relieved not to be the focal point. After making a plan to take me on a day trip to St. Adolphe, the town they had grown up in, Auntie Pat and her grandson left to run errands. For lunch, Maman and I had toasted tomato sandwiches, which, I was to learn, were a daily staple for her. Then we took a taxi to my brother's apartment.

When he opened the door and I looked into his smiling brown eyes, I saw myself mirrored. It wasn't so much the physical likeness but experiencing the presence of someone whose way of being in the world was much like mine. There was seamless harmony between his energy and my own; the sense of being kin with him was instantaneous. There was something about him that I had always known.

Is this what the bond between biological brothers and sisters feels like? Is it because we all grew from a cluster of cells in the same womb? Because we all started our lives in the same place, feeling our mother and hearing her cries as we made our way here? Because of the blood and blood memory that we share? Because there are things we know about each other that came to us before other kinds of conscious knowing?

Or in our case, was it because our connection to each other was unencumbered by the echo of abandonment? Because we had never chosen to leave one another? Because it was not by our doing that we ended up not knowing each other until we were in our thirties and forties? Because there was nothing unresolved between us but the unadulterated joy of finally breaching the distance that had kept us apart?

I spent the afternoon with the brother I had just met and my nephew. I've always read people's bookshelves and music collections as a way to get to know them, so I looked through my brother's CDs. I could have been looking through my own. This brother was an amazing bass player; we talked about our favourite bass riffs in some of the songs we both liked. And because I am always prepared for hanging out with kids, I had some origami paper with me and taught my nephew to fold paper cranes. Later, we picked up a friend of my brother's and went to the Forks to wander around. We passed some buskers drumming. It turned out that one of them was a friend of mine from my percussion community in Halifax. I sat in and jammed with them for a couple of tunes. My brother took some photos. We were a family out on the town on a summer afternoon.

# NIIZHOZIIBEAN—TWO RIVERS VI

My French ancestors were the bad boys for whom the rough, nascent cities of Trois-Rivières, Quebec, and Montreal were too refined. They came to this country for adventure in the wilderness, and they kept going farther and farther west to find it. From the seventeenth through to the nineteenth century, the canoes of the voyageurs were present on the Assiniboine and Red Rivers.

This was not to the liking of the Assiniboine people, who moved farther west and southwest themselves into what is now North Dakota and Montana. By the second half of the nineteenth century, European settlement began in earnest along the banks of the rivers—and the original people who were in relationship with those rivers were becoming fewer and farther between.

Some of their descendants married the newcomers and became the founding families of the Métis Nation, settling along the riverbanks. Long, narrow lots provided the Métis with access to the river, fertile black soil for growing wheat, oats, barley, and vegetables, and some land back from the river for pasture. These lots also allowed for proximity to neighbours, essential to our communal way of life. This way of sharing the land met the practical needs of transportation, irrigation, and communication since the river was still the main thoroughfare, and the growing season was hot and dry. After the Hudson's Bay Company sold these lands to the British Crown right out from under my ancestors, surveyors arrived from Ontario and tried to revise the apportioning of land using the square lots that were the norm there. Putting these surveyors on the run was one of the first acts of resistance of my people.

The Red River received its designation as a Canadian Heritage River in 2007. The Canadian Heritage Rivers System is administered by the federal, provincial, and territorial governments to conserve and protect rivers that provide the best examples of the historical and cultural role rivers have played in our country. The Sustainable Development agency of Manitoba is responsible for monitoring the well-being of the Red River. In its ten-year monitoring report published in 2018, it states that the Red has been "the site of numerous historical and cultural events."[23] One of the best known of those events involved my great-great-grandfather, Elzéar Goulet.

In 1869, Elzéar was a hardworking Métis man with a growing family, living in the bush not far from the Red River Settlement. He was the mail courier between the settlement and a community to the south known as Pembina. He travelled back and forth on the Crow Wing Trail, by dogsled in the winter and on horseback the rest of the year. "He was the Pony Express!" my mother told me, laughing.

Trouble was coming to the settlement. The government of John A Macdonald had tried to install a governor in the territory, but the Métis prevented William McDougall from coming in. Macdonald intended to annex the territory, which they called Rupert's Land, into Confederation and encourage more settlement. This plan did not go over well with those who already lived there. The Hudson's Bay Company not only presided over the fur trade but provided a form of civic government as well. The Métis felt that was as much government as they needed. When the company sold Rupert's Land to the colonial government, and surveyors arrived to stake out claims, a Métis militia began to take shape. Elzéar joined other men in the community who would ride over on horseback to tell the newcomers that the land they were marking off was already occupied. It was a logical step for Elzéar to become involved with Riel's provisional government. In fact, he was a natural leader and a favourite of Riel's, who made him second-in-command of the Métis militia at Fort Garry.

In the course of his duties, Elzéar participated in the arrest, detention, trial, and execution of Thomas Scott, a settler of Irish descent and an Orangeman. The Orangemen were infamous for their hatred of Catholics, the French, and Indigenous Peoples, which added up to three strikes against the Métis. After publicly and persistently boasting of his plan to murder Riel during the time of the provisional government,

Scott was charged with treason. Riel was not part of the military tribunal that tried Scott and found him guilty. In fact, it is said that he visited Scott in his cell and implored him to retract his stated intention to kill Riel, but to no avail. My great-great-grandfather, however, was a member of that tribunal, and of the firing squad that carried out the execution. Whatever one might think today of the decision to execute Scott, there is no doubt in my mind that my ancestor acted out of his commitment to protect our people and our homeland during a time of great unrest.

Meanwhile, John A. Macdonald, at the same time that he was pretending to negotiate with Riel on terms that would be acceptable to the Métis for our territory to become part of Canada, sent the Wolseley expedition, a force of two thousand British soldiers and volunteers, to put down what is referred to by the colonizers as the Red River Rebellion and by my people as the Red River Resistance. When knowledge of the approaching army reached Riel and the other members of the provisional government, they knew that the negotiations had been a sham and that they would be massacred if they stayed to try to hold the fort. The leaders of the provisional government dispersed, seeking safety in the short term but not losing sight of their long-term vision of self-government. Riel went into hiding, and others laid low, but Elzéar, for whatever reason—perhaps because he had a wife and five children to take care of, with a sixth on the way—went back to delivering the mail.

In September 1870, with Wolseley's men milling around the settlement, pumped up for a battle that never happened, Elzéar went into the Red Saloon in Winnipeg to pick up the mail to be delivered to Pembina. Inside, he was recognized by some of the soldiers, who shouted and gave chase, threatening to lynch him. My great-great-grandfather ran out and down the road (now Lombard Avenue) to the river, where he jumped in and began to swim across to the Saint Boniface side. The mob began throwing rocks at him, one of which hit him on the head and knocked him unconscious. He drowned. He was thirty-four years old. His body was recovered the following day. No charges were ever laid, nobody ever held accountable for his murder. His death marked the beginning of what has gone down in history as the Reign of Terror against the Red River Métis. If a Métis person showed their face on the west side of the river, they were in danger. Many of our people were beaten and raped.

In 2008, Parc Commémoratif Elzéar-Goulet was officially opened on the eastern bank of the Red River, where Elzéar would have reached safety had he not been killed in the attempt. The Elzéar Goulet Local of the Manitoba Métis Federation knew that I had written a song about him. I'd recorded it with my brother and my uncle, both musicians, on one of my visits home, and Maman had played it for them. They flew me in from Unama'ki to sing it at the opening ceremony and made it a surprise for Maman. Tears filled her eyes when I stepped out of my brother's car at the cemetery situated on the grounds of the Saint Boniface Cathedral. The event was to begin at Elzéar's grave. I gathered with my family and our community to listen to Métis fiddler Sierra Noble play the Warrior's Lament at Elzéar's graveside, then we walked down Avenue Taché as part of a large group of my people, our Métis flag flapping overhead.

The park occupies four hectares of land and was designed to reflect the tragic death of my great-great-grandfather. The flat ground has been sculpted to undulate like water, and large boulders have been placed here and there in memory of the way he was killed. The path through the park is in the shape of the infinity symbol that appears on our flag, representing two cultures coming together to create a Nation that will live forever. In the middle of the park, a low stone wall curves around the area where plaques tell his story, along with its significance in the history of my people and the founding of Manitoba. On the wall is etched a quote from Grandma describing her grandfather:

*Il fallait quelqu'un de très fort ... quelqu'un qui connaissait les chevaux. Un mecanicien et un réparateur né. Quelqu'un de prudent et qui soit conscient de ses responsabilités—assurer la livraison du courrier et des bagages à travers de si grandes distances ... un homme de confiance qui soit le bienvenu aux postes de relais qui étaient sur son chemin. Il devait faire prevue de modération et de ténacité.*

It took a person of great strength … He must know horses. He must be a born mechanic and repairman. He must be alert and conscious of his great charges—the delivery of papers and baggage throughout such great distances … He must be a trusted man, welcome at relay posts along the way. He must be temperate and enduring.

Elzéar's many qualities, written in stone.

When the speeches were over, it was time to sing my song. I stood there by the river, flanked on either side by two of my brothers, my hair and the ribbons on my regalia blowing in the summer breeze, my mother and my oldest sister listening in the crowd. It was one of the proudest moments of my life.

No family is perfect. My birth family, like so many families, contains a mix of love and pain, of strong bonds and broken relationships. Over time these have shifted as some fences are mended and as people drift apart or choose distance. The summer I met my family for the first time, a couple of my siblings who lived in Winnipeg were not in touch with our mother.

It was always a challenge to try to find a balance between respecting those siblings' choices and honouring my right to meet them all and make my own decisions. That first day with Maman, it was clear to me that she was nervous that I would be meeting my sister who lived in Winnipeg. She hinted that I would be told things about her that were not very nice. That was the closest she ever came to acknowledging her failings as a mother when my oldest five siblings were little kids. To say she neglected them in their early years does not adequately describe what went on. Eventually, they were apprehended by the local child welfare agency, separated, and sent to different foster homes. The brother who is the youngest of that five was adopted by a white couple who were cattle ranchers in northern Manitoba. He had a wonderful life with that family, unlike my other siblings.

I could see that there were family stories that my mother would never tell me because she wanted me to have a good opinion of her. I could also see that she was worried my siblings would tell me these stories. I told Maman what I told them all: I had missed out on knowing my family for close to half my life, and I wanted to meet and get to know them all on my own terms.

In the days before my trip to Winnipeg that summer, I had been asked by my friend Rita McKeough to help her out with one of her art projects. Rita is an installation artist whose works come from a seemingly boundless imagination. Before I met her, I experienced one of her pieces in a Halifax gallery: she had built a house that we walked through, listening to sounds coming through speakers embedded in the walls. The piece critiqued domestic violence against women; the house represented a home where a woman had been beaten. Working off the expression *if only these walls could speak*, Rita had given the walls voice. It was eerie and powerful.

I got to meet Rita in the 1980s, when we were teamed up for a direct action coordinated by the Halifax peace movement on August 6, the anniversary of the devastating detonation of a nuclear bomb in Hiroshima in 1945. Teams of three people each were equipped with spray paint and life-size stencils of human bodies of all ages and genders, then assigned to different areas of the city. We used the stencils and paint to create the outlines of human beings all over roads and sidewalks throughout the metro area, commemorating the obliteration of thousands of Japanese citizens who were vaporized on the spot in the midst of their daily activities. We met after dark and worked through the night. I remember Rita's red pickup truck. I remember thinking she was cool as dirt.

After that, Rita involved me as a singer in a couple more of her creations, including one in the summer of 1998, just before my trip to Winnipeg to meet my family. She was really happy for me and coincidentally would be heading there too to install her latest art piece in a location on the outskirts of the city. She asked if I had time before I left to record some vocals for it. Always glad to be involved in anything Rita was doing, I agreed to meet her in her studio on Barrington Street a few days before my flight out west. Rita explained that the sound recording I was contributing to would come from speakers mounted on tracks, moving back and forth on each side of the outdoor installation as the music played. She gave me a note as a starting point and asked me to riff on it in a minor key. It didn't take long, and we were both pleased with the outcome. We wished each other well in our respective summer adventures and said goodbye.

●-●-●

On the day I was to meet my oldest sister for the first time, I phoned her, and we made a plan to meet downtown. She is a well-known and highly respected visual artist in the Winnipeg arts community, and we were going to see some of her pieces at the Neeginan Centre, an Indigenous community centre located in the old Canadian Pacific Railway station on North Main. But first, we were going to meet outside the coffee shop where my nephew was working so I could meet him too.

I arrived at the address in Winnipeg's trendy Exchange District at the agreed-upon time. I had no trouble recognizing my sister from the photos I had seen. She was tall, a statuesque beauty.

We embraced, then stood on the sunny sidewalk in the glow of the moment, beginning a conversation that would continue for years.

My sister suggested we go inside so I could meet her son. We entered the coffee shop and I saw him, the barista on duty behind the counter, busy serving a customer. In that same glance, I saw my friend Rita. Before I could ask her what she was doing there, she grinned from ear to ear, rubbed my arm, and exclaimed over and over, "Look who your sister is! Look who your sister is!"

My world imploded. I was completely disoriented and overwhelmed. Looking back, I hope my nephew felt how happy I was to meet him. He served me coffee as time and space collapsed and what I had thought were completely separate parts of my life came together in front of my eyes, forming a fascinating and beautiful scene.

Not only did my sister and Rita know each other, they had collaborated on artworks in the past. In fact, my sister had sewn the costumes that the performers would wear to bring to life Rita's newest installation— the same one I'd made the recording for before leaving on that trip.

My sister and I worked on the same art project before we even met.

From that astounding beginning, we shared so much: our political perspectives on the depth and breadth of the damage caused by colonization, the power of cultural practices to heal us, a love of being in the bush and harvesting traditional medicines, a passion for singing and drumming. A few days later, she took me to a ceremony, where she invited me to sing with her. I learned my first Anishinaabe song that day: the Wolf Song. Wolf is a teacher, running some distance in front of the pack to bring back knowledge of what lies ahead. My oldest sister was my first teacher in the traditional ways of my people. I could not have hoped for more.

*Ma'iingan abindige, ma'iingan abindiga.*

Wolf, come in.

# WHEN MY SISTER DRUMS

When my sister drums
Sparks fly from her eyes
And her smile lights the day
Like a million suns rising

When my sister drums
A lost child's cries
Become one with the song
And carry her along
To where the rivers meet
And the sacred heartbeat
Keeps us strong

Standing with my sister in the circle
This is what I came here for
Drumming with the women in the circle
Like so many women have before

When my sister drums
She returns to those rivers
Running like the veins
In the body of the mother
Who has never left us
We have known no other
Her waters refresh us
Heal us and bless us

When my sister drums
Her pain splits the air
True as any arrow
Anywhere
From there to here
It flies through fear
When my sister drums

Truth comes

# TWO-SPIRITS?

With Maman beside me in the passenger seat, I drove down the main street of Beausejour, past the sprawling co-op grocery store and the iconic Beausejour bowling alley. Fading red paint on the brick facade read *Beausejour Lanes,* while a modern neon sign stating the same was tacked on underneath like a flashy afterthought. Although it was a bright July morning, I could picture the sign spilling a red glow over the entrance on a Friday night. We drove past the yards of modest small-town bungalows with their midseason gardens and out the other end of town, past the water tower and the grain elevators, until the deep yellow of canola and dense jungles of corn flanked us on either side.

We turned onto a dirt road and soon arrived at the Dr. Jessie Saulteaux Resource Centre, gravel crunching under the tires as we pulled into a parking spot. Maman and I got out and stretched for a minute before asking the first person who walked by where we needed to go to register for the Two-Spirit Gathering.

I had come out in my early twenties, first identifying as a lesbian, then as bisexual. I'd found all the terms in use in the eighties and nineties not quite right for me. In fact, even the term *sexual orientation* seemed to reduce my self-understanding to a matter of who my sexual partners were. When I reconnected with my culture, I breathed a sigh of relief. I was Two-Spirited. Yes.

The term *Two-Spirited* is said to have been adopted at an international gathering of Indigenous queer folks in Winnipeg in 1990 and has come to be used widely throughout Turtle Island. What I liked about the term was that it refers to spirit *and* sexuality and gender, not just sex. Prior to the evolution of consciousness that has brought about our critique of the gender binary, the term *Two-Spirited* was intended to be used by individuals who felt they carried both a masculine and feminine spirit. That felt right to me at that point in my life.

The reason for my trip to Winnipeg that summer was meeting my family, but I tucked into the back of my mind that the gathering, which moves around from province to province, was happening in Manitoba that year. It was only a forty-minute drive from Winnipeg, and Uncle Derry was willing to lend me his car. Spending time with my Métis family was my priority, but I also hoped to take in some of the gathering.

I had decided long before the day I first met Maman that I was going to come out to her right away. Having gone through the agonizing process of deciding if, when, and how to come out to my adoptive family years earlier, I was not willing to go back into the closet when getting to know my birth family. So I came out to my birth mother the day after we met. She was unfazed. She told me she thought one of my sisters who had died before we reconnected had been gay. The two of them had been close. Maman had always hoped my sister would find a relationship that made her happy but felt she never had. Maman was open and accepting, and we didn't skip a beat. In fact, she agreed to come to the Two-Spirit Gathering with me.

Together, we wandered around the beautiful grounds, meeting people. Maman connected with another mother, a Cree woman who was there to support her son. We attended workshops, listened to Elders speak, and learned some Medicine Wheel teachings. And we had fun! We had a great time sitting around with people and introducing ourselves as mother and daughter, then telling our new friends that we had met only two days ago just to see the looks on their faces.

I guess not having had the opportunity to have a relationship for the first thirty-eight years of my life put things into perspective for us. We had nothing to lose and everything to gain. After a day of hanging out with a group of people who had long ago figured out that love is the most important thing, we drove back to the city under the expansive darkness of the prairie sky.

These days I just prefer to say I'm queer. I'm playing with using the term *Indigiqueer*, first coined by filmmaker Thirza Cuthand and adopted by author Joshua Whitehead. It has the spaciousness of being non-binary while not losing the distinctiveness of being Indigenous. Prior to colonization, both my Anishinaabe ancestors and the Mi'kmaq upon whose territory I now live had terms in their own languages for gender diverse community members. These did not always have to do with sexual orientation. In Anishinaabemowin, the term *niizh manidoowag* translates into "Two-Spirits" and referred to community members whose bodies housed both a masculine and a feminine spirit. In Mi'kmaw, *ji'nmue'sm kesalatl* means "he loves men."

After the colonizers arrived with their missionaries, *niizh manidooag* was replaced with *berdache*, which has linguistic roots in Italian, Spanish, and French and refers to "a person who engages in sodomy" and "a boy kept by a man who likes to have sex with boys." It was adopted by anthropologists to describe Indigenous individuals who dressed in the clothing of the opposite sex. It's a derogatory term. In Mi'kma'ki, the same thing happened; the gender diverse members of the community began to be called *puoin*, which prior to Christianity meant "a person who communicates with the unseen" but was reinterpreted by the priests to mean "the devil" and is now considered pejorative. It's important for us to stay connected to the history of diverse sexual and gender identities in our many Indigenous nations and how the community members who identified in these ways and the language used to refer to them were demonized by Christian missionaries, who were key agents of colonization. The annual Two-Spirit Gathering is about decolonizing the language and honouring ourselves as part of the continuum of traditions and the teachings of our ancestors.

Language is powerful. Even when it is not spoken, it lives in our minds and shapes how we think in ways we are often unaware of. The words available to us to speak about who we are, about whom and how we love, create invisible frameworks that affect our understanding of ourselves and others. Sometimes those frameworks create boxes that many of us have to work really hard to break out of. Both the words we do have and the words we don't have contribute to this. As the mother of a trans individual, it is important to me to liberate the way I think and the language I use. Misgendering people hurts them. So I now question the term *Two-Spirited*. To me, it used to feel freeing and all-encompassing; now I worry it reinforces the gender binary that limits our capacity to accept and love ourselves and others.

# SONGS AND A NAME

When I was preparing for the trip home to meet my birth family, I knew that I wanted to learn some of the traditional songs my people sing, though I didn't know who could teach me or help make this happen. When I met my sister that summer, I knew she would be the one.

She was a member of what was then called the North End Women's Centre Drum Group (now the NEWC Buffalo Gals Drum Group). She called up a friend from the drum group and told her about my request. They arranged a time for the friend to come over and meet with me.

A couple of days later, my sister's friend arrived at her house in the early afternoon. She took out her medicine bundle and set her sacred objects and medicines on a small table in front of her. I sat on the couch perpendicular to the little table in a state of deep respect and anticipation. I found out at the end of our time together that day that she was a member of the Midewiwin Lodge, a sacred society within Anishinaabe culture that maintains social, spiritual, and healing practices of the Nation. We began with smudging; the rich scent of sage filled the living room, making clouds in the stream of sunlight filtering in through the curtains. I sat silently in the sacred space, and we prayed. After a while, she spoke, her voice as quiet as the summer afternoon. She was going to teach me two songs. The first was a song I could sing anytime, anywhere.

*Miigwech, Gitchi Manitou*
*Miigwech, Gitchi Manitou*
*Way ha, a way ha, a way ha, way a ho*

(Thank you, Great Spirit)

I listened with rapt attention as she sang. After a bit, I joined in. Before long, we were singing it together.

The second song I was only to sing in the lodge, in ceremony. It was also an expression of gratitude, thanking Creator for this good life—*pimatisiwin* in Cree. Again, I listened and then sang along until I knew it. Singing these songs felt like coming home after a long, long time away.

Learning these particular songs was my first teaching about gratitude, a core value in Indigenous world view and spirituality. Every time we pray, we begin with gratitude. First thing in the morning, we express our gratitude for the gift of being alive another day. At the beginning of a gathering or a meeting, we express gratitude for the opportunity to be together. No matter the occasion, we give thanks to Creator. We never make a request to Creator in our prayers without expressing gratitude first. The gift I received that afternoon was not only the two new songs, which I would carry with me for the rest of my life, but also this fundamental teaching. It has stayed with me and guided me every day since.

My teacher emphasized that I was not to write down the words to the songs. I was so worried I would forget what I had learned that after she left, I sang the two songs over and over again for the rest of the day. I have never forgotten them in the twenty-five years that have passed.

As our time together that day drew to a close, my teacher started to put away her medicine bundle. Without saying a word, she gave me a small, flat piece of dark-grey shale on which was painted a green turtle. I thanked her. This small painted stone became part of my bundle; I carry it everywhere. After telling me a couple more things about the spiritual path ahead for me, she left, her quiet presence lingering.

●-●-●

Another of my spiritual teachers, Mi'kmaw Elder and Pipe Carrier Jane Meader, learned to lead ceremony with Diane Longboat, a Haudenosaunee Pipe Carrier from the territory of the Six Nations of the Grand River in Ontario. Once, when Diane was visiting here in Unama'ki, my son and I were invited to a Naming Ceremony at Jane's home.

A person's Spirit Name is the name they had before they were born. We come into the world with this name; even if we are not aware of it, it is the name by which Creator and our ancestors in the Spirit World know us. When we receive our Spirit Name in ceremony, we know who we are. It deepens our self-understanding, strengthens our connection and communication with Spirit, and provides guidance and protection.

My son and I and another mother and her daughter sat in the middle of a circle formed by Jane, Diane, and some members of Jane's family. The two Pipe Carriers smudged their bundles and pipes, then smoked their pipes while praying to the seven directions. One of the others drummed throughout. After the pipe ceremony was completed, Diane gave each of us our Spirit Name, our medicine—the gifts we carry that we are meant to share in this lifetime—and our colours.

That was how I came to understand the significance of the little piece of shale that had been given to me nine years earlier.

My Spirit Name is Green Turtle Woman.

there's a knowledge we can't speak
it lives behind our eyes
we feel it rise
skies
darkened by *kitpu's*[24] wings
and in this dark
we see such things
as light can never show

there's a knowledge we can't speak
it lives beneath our feet
receives
believes
each step we take
with steady
readiness
holds and breaks
the fall
of all that is not real
reveals the path
we can't yet see
but only know
by the feel
and flow
of this day

*E'e*[25]

this is the way

# ANOTHER BROTHER

I was told from the start that I had another brother. Although not related to us by blood, my sisters and brothers were insistent that I would not have met the whole family until I met him.

This I could understand.

Family as it is commonly understood has always been a bit of an alien concept to me. A shifty thing, like squinting in a fog, where any source of light actually obscures what you're trying to see.

I had two mothers, and both had rejected me. Without that mooring, I was perpetually adrift.

But a brother who was not related by blood or legal papers but was absolutely our brother?

That was easy to grasp.

# NIAGARA FALLS

I waited almost a year to meet you, to
scan the arrivals area in another airport
for a face I'd been told
looked a lot like mine

what spilled from us in those tears?
what old wounds and unmet needs wet our faces?
what rusty hinges creaked as ancient
doors opened
lighting dark rooms of loss?

small talk rested precariously
on a mix of hope that tasted like childhood
fear seasoned by disappointment
faith made reckless by an impulse whose
source was a distant past
I leaned forward
straining against my seat belt in the back seat
to be closer to you as we talked
the front passenger seat occupied by the friend you'd brought along
your fortitude for navigating the QEW and 400-series highways

we traversed many distances to find
each other
we reached across the years
from across your kitchen table

when we tried to go back to where we both started
when I asked about the childhood I had missed
you would stare off somewhere
to a place I had never been
a place it seemed you didn't like to remember
I teeter-tottered
wanting to know
not wanting to cause you pain

you were brave
making forays into those lost years
to retrieve something to
bring back and show me:
*you would have loved Grandma*
*she always dressed us up and made us feel special*
then hurrying back to the present
safer here
against the backdrop of domestic life with a husband
three sons still at home
a cat and a dog
we were just sisters hanging out
for the first time
passing the timelessness with daily outings
tea runs and yard sales
window-shopping at the chic shops in the touristy part of town
ending up at the second-hand store tucked away on a side street
sighing our relief in tandem to be back
on familiar ground
drives along the canal
smelling the freshness of the lake
the acrid scent of diesel and wet concrete
rising up like the looming lake boats
back in town
teenagers jumped off the high cement walls of the canal
splashing into the water
their cries a canticle of
universal joy

looking out at Niagara Falls
standing side by side at the railing
one of the seven wonders of the world

# IT'S NOT WHO YOU CLAIM,
# IT'S WHO CLAIMS YOU

When I found my birth family and learned that I was Métis, I was only able to follow my heart back to my homeland for short visits. I had a child whose father lived in Mi'kma'ki, and although we were not in a relationship, I didn't need a family court judge to tell me that I could not move to Manitoba. I wanted my son's father to be part of his life. I knew it was an important part of our child's well-being, and I respected his rights as a father. We agreed to co-parent; he was present at the birth, and he spent time with our child on a regular basis.

However, I also knew that I needed to connect with Indigenous people and community. While still living in Halifax, I volunteered at Healing Our Nations, an organization that began as the Atlantic First Nations AIDS Task Force. Another example of the synchronicity that has been present throughout my process of reconnecting with my family and culture: I had been hired by a Mi'kmaw colleague to write the grant proposal that secured the funding to establish this place. I had played a role in bringing into existence a Mi'kmaw organization that, unbeknownst to me at the time, would eventually be there for me when I needed a way to connect with Indigenous community.

A few hours a week was not enough though. I wanted to immerse myself in Indigenous culture. I began to look for jobs as a therapist in a Mi'kmaw community. A friend told me about an opening in We'koqma'q First Nation. I applied for the position in the summer of 2003.

But there was a problem. It was a contract for only eight months— the amount of time needed for the person already in the job to go back to Ontario and complete her master's degree at a university there. It didn't make sense for me, a single mother with a four-year-old, to uproot my child and myself from the community of young families we were part of in St. Margaret's Bay, on the outskirts of Halifax, for a contract job. Against my better judgment, I went for it anyway.

I got an interview, which took place on a hot day in late August in a coffee shop in Chéticamp. Fortunately, a family from the city who I was friends with were staying at a summer home in a village just south of there. They offered me a place to stay the night before and agreed to watch my little one while I went to the interview.

I arrived at the coffee shop and spotted the health director who was going to interview me. I sat down, took a breath, and began to answer her questions. My master's degree in counselling had not included any training in Indigenous mental health, but I at least had some awareness of what I was lacking. I knew there were significant cultural differences, though I did not know the extent of those differences at the time. My experiences working in street culture, as well as the African Nova Scotian community, had grounded me in humility and respect, crucial qualities in cross-cultural work that the health director recognized. I understood the importance of knowing the limits of my understanding. I still believe that knowing what we *don't* know is the most important aspect of a respectful approach when working in a culture that is not our own. This, combined with my seven years of experience working as a therapist in Halifax, led the health director to offer me the job on the spot.

I did not accept right away but asked for a few days to think about it. I was butterflies-in-my-stomach excited about the opportunity, but at the same time, I was more than a little daunted by the huge undertaking of finding a place for me and my child to live, arranging child care, and getting us moved out of our charming Seabright cottage and into our new rental in the few weeks before I was to start my new job.

I picked my son up from our friends' place and decided to take a longer way home, turning inland at Inverness and cutting across the island, a route that meant driving through We'koqma'q. My child, who was already a road warrior due to all the trips back and forth between our home and his dad's, was happily ensconced in his car seat in the back, listening to a favourite cassette, leaving me free to pray—which I did, fervently, the whole way. I asked Creator for guidance, reflecting on the work involved in the move and the insanity of going through all that for a short-term contract. I thought about my desire to help Indigenous people heal from the deep wounds of colonization and how, even though I wouldn't be working with my own Nation, I could learn more about Indigenous cultures if I made this move. I was full of passion and uncertainty in equal parts. I asked Creator to give me a sign. I was in Unama'ki, bald eagle country. I thought if I saw an eagle, I would know that I should accept the job offer. I scanned the sky as much as I could while still keeping my eyes on the road.

I did not see an eagle.

When I arrived at the intersection of Highway 395 and the Trans-Canada, in the settler village of Whycocomagh (an anglicized version of We'koqma'q), I pulled in to a gas station and gazed at the small Mi'kmaw community nestled in the hills to my right. Then, the most amazing thing happened. The cassette tape ended and popped itself out of the deck, and CBC Radio came on. I felt disoriented as I heard myself and my Four the Moment sisters coming through the speakers. CBC was playing one of our tunes. Our recordings got some airplay on the radio from time to time, though not often.

I heard us singing: *"In my soul, I know we will come through."*

I took the job.

Identity is understood differently in different cultures. The Eurocentric concept of self, for example, is dominant in colonial Canada. It centres notions of individual agency—the "everyone can pull themselves up by their bootstraps and make something of themselves if they want to" ideology, the "if I can do it, so can you" rhetoric. Among the problems with this way of thinking are the ways it masks systemic inequity and allows hierarchical institutions to perpetuate themselves, unquestioned, and the ways it generates internalized shame, blame, and guilt among structurally disadvantaged and marginalized peoples. These are the values and beliefs that I intuitively rejected as a little girl. As a teenager, I used my connection to the Catholic Church—specifically liberation theology and its call for social justice—as a portal into critical thinking about the world I grew up in. It was the only door available to me at the time, and it led me to leave Catholicism and its stubborn adherence to patriarchal power behind.

However, it wasn't until I arrived in We'koqma'q and met the Elders who would become my teachers and mentors that I found another way of understanding myself and the rest of the human family. It was then I realized that in some cultures, the self is understood to be both collective and ecocentric.

For Indigenous Peoples, the self is inseparable from the community. A person is not only themselves but also a family member, a community member, and a member of their nation, all at the same time. These are not aspects of life that we give separate time and attention to in turn, as members of the dominant culture might think. This is who we are, always, at every moment, in every context. Our interconnectedness and the wholeness that comes with that are sacred. I learned from the Elders that relationship is at the centre of everything, including how we understand ourselves.

I also learned that we source our identity from the land and that our languages hold and carry this understanding. The land is so much more than our physical location. The land is a network of relationships that have existed since time before memory. Mother Earth and all the life She supports are to be loved and cared for in the same way She cares for us. When we see the land, we see mythology and sacredness, as well as food that sustains us physically and spiritually. The web of relationships we experience on the land is the same web of relationships that sustained our ancestors; the teachings that guide our relationships with the land have been passed down from them and are a constant connection with those who have gone before us. We know who we are through our life on the land. We experience the continuity of our lineage and our culture on the land.

The centrality of these relationships with community and the land are core teachings of all the Indigenous cultures I have learned about so far. Through our cultures, which are connected to our home territories at their core, we know who we are, who we belong to, where we came from, and how to relate to one another, including All Our Relations in the natural world. No'koqma'q' is the Mi'kmaw word for this; in Anishinaabemowin it is *gidinawendimin*; in Cree, *wahkohtowin*. All of life has a Spirit and is sacred; this belief informs all our ways of knowing and being.

I did not know these things about what it means to be Indigenous before I arrived in We'koqma'q. I knew bits and pieces. Before I consciously knew that I was Métis, I had learned as much as I could about Indigenous rights and taken action in solidarity with land claim and sovereignty struggles across the country, even forming a group with some settler activists called Nova Scotians in Solidarity with Native Peoples. We built relationships with folks in the Mi'kmaw community and organized educational events for non-Indigenous people who wanted to take supportive action on Indigenous issues. But the result of growing up white was that I still unconsciously saw the world and the issues through a colonial lens. I had to be immersed in community where I was embraced and challenged, encouraged and taught, and I had to be adopted—this time informally and much more meaningfully—through a profoundly loving relationship with Elder Caroline Gould, whom I called Auntie Caroline, before I could understand what it means to be Indigenous.

There is ongoing debate about how to define Indigenous identity. This is one of the many legacies of colonization we are still working through. It is not easy to decolonize our minds and spirits and return to our original ways of knowing. We have inherited the reserve system and the Indian Act and have no choice but to be in some kind of relationship with the colonial government that still has so much control over our lives. Part of that control is exercised through government definitions of who is and isn't Indigenous, and to what degree. This is yet another colonial strategy that enables governments to dodge honouring their treaty obligations: they posit that they cannot proceed with treaty negotiations until we can be clear about who is and is not a member of our nations. The confusion they have created serves them well.

The United Nations Permanent Forum on Indigenous Issues has come up with a number of points that form a modern understanding of Indigenous identity.

- Self-identification as indigenous peoples at the individual level and accepted by the community as their member
- Historical continuity with pre-colonial and/or pre-settler societies
- Strong link to territories and surrounding natural resources

- Distinct social, economic or political systems
- Distinct language, culture and beliefs
- Form non-dominant groups of society
- Resolve to maintain and reproduce their ancestral environments and systems as distinctive peoples and communities[26]

The first point is foundational. According to our ways of knowing, you can't be Indigenous without a community. Niigaan Sinclair, an associate professor of Indigenous Studies at the University of Manitoba from Peguis First Nation, wrote in his column in the *Winnipeg Free Press*: "It's not about who you claim but who claims you."[27]

When I started looking for work in a Mi'kmaw community, what I consciously understood was that I needed more *information* about Indigenous cultures. This was evidence of the colonial, Eurocentric concepts of knowledge and understanding I had been immersed in with my white adoptive family. I didn't yet understand that I needed to experience Indigenous community in order to know myself as an Indigenous person. I was following an inner compass that had been calibrated by blood memory, beyond the scope of cognitive knowing. On my first day in that new job, a prominent Elder in the community came to meet me, and it was obvious that her priority was checking out my heart, not my degrees or years of experience. I knew immediately that working in We'koqma'q was going to be a transformative experience. It thrilled me to receive this teaching: my work in this community was going to be heart centred. This is my natural way of being, and it was invited and welcomed in as the core aspect of the service I would be providing, no professional persona necessary. As the years went on, I understood more and more deeply that I needed to be part of an Indigenous community in order to know who I was. I believe the unconscious knowledge that is blood memory brought me there.

Looking at identity issues through an Indigenous lens raises the spectre of the tragedy of cultural loss sustained through dislocation from and destruction of Indigenous communities. We have to grapple with difficult questions that the widespread multi-dimensional impacts of colonization have laid at our feet. Many displaced Indigenous people wonder how they can ever reclaim and reconnect with who they are.

For people like me, it has been and continues to be difficult but doable, at least in some ways. I was able to reunite with a family and a community that was still alive and committed to old and new ways of living and thriving on our Métis homeland. Family members and my community welcomed me back and helped me to reconnect, asserting in no uncertain terms that I was one of them. Although I was geographically dislocated because of the Sixties Scoop and my need to get away from where I grew up, I was able to find an Indigenous community, albeit in another nation, that embraced me and shared teachings that were fundamentally similar to teachings in my own Métis Nation. I know that this has been a huge blessing in my life and that my experience is not typical for most of us who lost our families, communities, and cultures through the Sixties Scoop.

What about Sixties Scoop survivors, residential school survivors, and the disproportionate number of our children in the child welfare system who have not been able to reconnect with family and community? What about Indigenous individuals from places where their ancestral communities were almost or completely destroyed so that there is no community to return to and reconnect with?

Colonization, its nasty tentacles reaching into so many aspects of our lives, has really messed with our ability to know who we are. But that does not take away from the importance of creating relationships within community for those of us who lost that connection in any of the many ways it occurs. Sinclair states, "Being Indigenous has a little to do with blood and ancestry, but has far more to do with the relationships one builds and embodies."[28]

My experience has reinforced this teaching. My lineage alone—though powerful, inspiring, and grounding—would not have been enough to help me find my feet as an Indigenous woman in the world. In the ways of knowing that are grounded in the world view of the Métis Nation, sourced from our Cree and Anishinaabe ancestors, the concept of the self is collective. In reclaiming my Métis identity, I must accept that this world view shapes who I am. Therefore, I cannot know who I am without community.

In conversations with other culturally displaced Indigenous individuals who have not connected with Indigenous community—

their community of origin or any other—yet still want to identify as Indigenous, I have heard things like, "But community can be hard." To which I can only reply, Of course it's hard! All First Nations, Inuit, and Métis individuals and communities in what is now called Canada have been wounded and are at different places in our healing journeys. There is also ongoing racism, one manifestation of which is the cultural appropriation evident in race shifting, now sometimes called Indigenous identity fraud—yet another colonial practice that exploits and steals from us. What is left for them to take? Our Indigenous identities.

The result is justified mistrust, often the first thing a person encounters when trying to make relationships in our communities. One must take the perspective of *kitpu*, the Mi'kmaw word for "eagle," who from their vantage point high in the sky can see the big picture, to put in context the lack of warmth and friendliness, check in with one's humility and respect, ground oneself in the knowledge that it's probably not personal (unless we're acting like entitled assholes), and keep trying. Taking this perspective also helps us to understand that when we reconnect with the beauty and power of our cultures and traditional teachings, we also reconnect with the suffering. To expect one without the other is to hang on to privilege, which forms a barrier to trust and relationship.

Gary Hines, music director of the African American musical group Sounds of Blackness, wrote a concise and powerful line about the cultural appropriation experienced in Black communities in his song "Livin' the Blues": "Everybody wanna sing my blues, nobody wanna live my blues."[29]

Community is where we experience it all. Community takes me to the depths of myself, inspires me in immeasurable life-giving ways, stretches the breadth of my capacity for love and resistance and healing and humour, and yes, sometimes it brings me to my knees. Community grounds me in who I am as an Indigenous woman.

By the time I arrived in We'koqma'q to begin my job as a community-based therapist, the person I was filling in for had decided not to finish her degree; the job was mine for as long as I wanted it. I stayed in that position for fifteen years. I have since left to write and work part-time as a therapist in private practice, but I continue to work primarily with Indigenous individuals. I still facilitate the We'koqma'q Residential School Survivors group and drum and sing with community members, many of whom have become family.

I guess that in my soul, I had known everything would work out.

Discovering a huge immediate and extended Métis family expanded my heart and my life in ways I could never have imagined. Getting to know them filled the weeks and months following that amazing summer of 1998, and I took numerous trips to Winnipeg to see them in the ensuing years.

On one of those trips in the autumn of 1999, with my three-month-old baby in tow, I ventured north to meet the brother who had also been adopted. That adoption had taken him 320 kilometres north of Winnipeg to a cattle ranch near the town of Rorketon that he eventually inherited from his adoptive parents. Driving up there through the hours and hours of flatlands Manitoba is famous for, I had plenty of time to think. Who was this guy, the second last of all the siblings I was to meet? I'd been told he almost never came into the city, as reclusive and mysterious as Manipogo, the sea monster said to lurk in the depths of Lake Manitoba, which was about an hour away from his home. I guided Uncle Derry's car farther and farther north on the grid of highways, making right-angle turns at intersections that appeared out of nowhere. On either side of the road were expansive fields that had been harvested earlier in the season, interspersed with stands of poplar and spruce, some occurring naturally and some planted as windbreaks by farmers wise to the fierce Manitoba winters.

I turned off the secondary highway onto the dirt road that led to my brother's house, driving alongside a line of trees until a gap opened up into a yard with a couple of sheds and a modest bungalow. As I pulled into the yard, a bearded man in jeans, a plaid cotton shirt with rolled-up sleeves, and unlaced workboots came out onto the step to greet me. I got my first look at the third of my four brothers. Deep-set brown eyes glinted out of a face that was tanned and creased, the face of a man who spent most of his time outdoors, no matter the weather. A ball cap on his head, his long, wavy brown hair framing a face that, while warm and friendly, also conveyed that he was a man who brooked no bullshit. I bounded up the steps into his outstretched arms, and soon we were laughing and shaking our heads in disbelief and joy. Minutes later, I was in his kitchen, sitting at the red Arborite table. While he made us coffee, I looked around. Heavy jackets bulged on wall hooks by the door, workboots and rubber boots were scattered on pieces of cardboard on the floor, farm smells mingled with the promising aroma of something in the oven that his mother had sent over for us.

Unlike my siblings who had survived foster care, my brother's adoption experience had been pretty great; he had nothing but love and gratitude for his adoptive parents. He'd been raised on this ranch and grown up wedded to the land. Although he no longer raises livestock for a living, at the time we first met, he had a couple hundred head of cattle. He was as rooted on that land as if he had sprouted up from it. The strength of his bond with the natural world—the land, the sky, the animals—radiated from him.

After we finished our coffee and the first round of sharing stories, we headed out to bring in the herd for the night, walking down a long dirt road to a pasture out back, my son in a Snugli carrier, lulled to sleep by the rhythm of my walking. My brother called the cows, and we turned around and started walking back toward the house. I could hear the low thundering of hundreds of hooves coming closer behind us. I looked nervously over my shoulder, and my brother laughed at me, amused by my fear of being trampled. I have always wanted to be like those cool farmer types completely unfazed by the size and formidable power of the animals they work with, but I've always fallen short of this aspiration. My rancher brother was all that and more, with an easy affinity between him and the cows. I guess growing up around them had led them to an understanding of each other. The humans who care for these huge creatures can read them so well, picking up on cues and messages most of us miss completely. He is as pragmatic as they come, yet my brother's love for the animals in his care was obvious. I loved seeing him in his element, witnessing his deep relationships with all the life around him.

I went back for another visit a few years later, met my sister-in-law, and heard more of the complicated story of her entry into our family. She told me that she and my brother were soulmates, and I could feel the truth of that. She toured me around her spectacular garden before the sun went down, and we spent the evening around the kitchen table, talking late into the night. I saw a bit more of the area the next day, when my niece took my son and me to the lake for a swim. On the morning we left, my brother—whose day began before dawn—left the house hours before the rest of us were up. It was still haying season. With directions from my sister-in-law, I tracked him down and walked across the fragrant, newly mown field to say goodbye. He bent down to grab a handful of hay and held it to his nose. He took a deep breath and sighed.

On each trip, I met more relatives and Elders and attended more and more community events. I drank in the music and the jigging, the joking and the politics, ate bison burgers and bannock. I checked out the Red River cart my mother had made with her Elders group that they would drive all the way from Pembina, North Dakota, to Winnipeg on the Crow Wing Trail, timing their arrival at the Forks to coincide with the opening ceremony of the North American Indigenous Games, which would be hosted in Winnipeg the summer of 2002.

The first several years after finding my mother were spent getting to know my family and my Métis community.

At some point in those first few years, I began to think more about my ancestors. I had heard a bit about each of them. I'd even gone to an exhibit at the museum run by the St. Boniface Historical Society, one of the founders of which was my great-grandfather, Roger Goulet. That exhibit featured my grandmother, Marie Thérèse Goulet Courchaine, as one of the prominent "femmes du Manitoba" in the history of the province. The more I learned, the more I wanted to know. As I moved through the process of getting to know my living relatives, I had more space in my heart and mind to think about the family members who had gone before me. Because I come from generations of prominent leaders, educators, and artists, there has been a great deal written about them. I found myself wondering what each of them would have to say to me about what it meant to be Métis. I decided to contemplate them each in turn with that question in my heart.

I started with my great-great-grandfather, Elzéar Goulet. I read as much as I could and thought about him a lot. I sent my question into the Spirit World: *If you were here now, what would you want me to understand about our people?* I began to hear him in my thoughts and in the liminal space between sleeping and waking. Words surfaced that seemed to be coming from him. Sometimes I had to get out of bed to write them down. How he had seen young Louis Riel grow into a leader, really sealing that fate when Louis returned from his studies in Quebec, confident and well spoken, having decided not to become a priest—at the time, the only reason a young man from the Northwest would go away to college. How Elzéar had realized that Louis was a young man to watch, that he would be the one to speak for our people. How indignant Elzéar had been when settler surveyors began staking claims for homesteads on lands already in use by Métis families. How our people have always resisted being governed by anything but the laws of nature, the dictates of the seasons, and the rules of the buffalo hunt.

When I felt that Elzéar had said what he wanted to say, I turned to his wife, Hélène Jérôme, *dit*[30] Saint-Matte.[31] I knew she had given birth to six children, the youngest not yet born when Elzéar was murdered by off-duty Canadian soldiers in 1870. She had lived a lot of the time as a single mother in the bush during the years her husband was away, working as the mail carrier in the region. After he died, she and the children had to leave their home in the bush and move to Saint Boniface to live with one of her brothers-in-law. Again, as I read about her life, it was as if she was speaking to me herself. I wrote down what I "heard": how much she'd loved their homestead and how capable she'd been of running it with the children while Elzéar was away for weeks at a time. How she'd known he was a leader who would be recognized and targeted by Canadian soldiers after the provisional government disbanded and the other leaders went into hiding, even though he was too humble to see it himself. How her heart had risen in her throat when a messenger arrived on horseback, knowing that it could only mean bad news. How she'd hated leaving that home to move in with Elzéar's brother Roger's family in Saint Boniface but knew she had no choice if she and the children were to survive.

I explored and experienced their son, Roger Goulet, in the same way, as if I were enjoying a visit over a cup of tea in the nursing home in Montreal where he'd lived at the end of his life, encouraged to move there by one of his sons who was a journalist in that city.

And then I came to his daughter, my grandmother, Marie Thérèse Goulet Courchaine. Grandma spoke so clearly to me. I felt how her great intellectual curiosity and love of meeting people of all backgrounds was rooted in a deep love of our Métis culture. Her fierce pride in being Métis had never wavered, not even during the years when most Manitoba Métis who could pass as Franco-Manitoban chose to do so in order to avoid racism—which has been present in Winnipeg from the days of John A. Macdonald right up to now. When I "gave her the floor," she chose to speak not only to me but to anyone who would listen about the importance of knowing who we are, where we come from, how we all have a story, and how our pride in all this can make us sturdier in the world.

In the end, I had four monologues. As I reread them, I found they were coherent narratives that needed almost no revision. They were like channelled writing. I had been merely a scribe as each spoke to me in turn over a period of just over a year.

I had plans to go to a winter solstice gathering in December 2002. I wanted to share these stories that were so inspiring to me, in keeping with the proverb that happiness shared is doubled. I was in an expansive space and could not keep my joy to myself. I contacted the hosts and asked if I could present the pieces, envisioning a dramatized recitation of some kind. My hosts welcomed the offer, and I began to memorize the first piece.

Then life interfered: a couple of weeks before the solstice, I was in a serious car accident in which my car was totalled. My injuries and the logistics of getting another car on the road made it impossible for me to memorize the monologues. I held a staged reading instead.

The response on that cold, dark night was heartwarming. The gut feeling I'd had that these stories would be inspiring to other people as well turned out to be true. That would have been the end of it, except that one of the audience members was a choreographer and dancer well connected in the Halifax theatre scene. Her feedback was more specific: she thought this work would be a great fit for the Halifax Fringe Festival and suggested I engage a director to help me turn it into a one-woman show. Even better, she offered to do some preliminary work with me to develop my ability to physically embody each of my predecessors. I had no theatre experience other than a high school drama class and a few amateur productions, but I was intrigued.

We met in a dance space on Grafton Street, and she taught me so much. She helped me to use my understanding of each of my four ancestors to identify where in their bodies each one felt centred. I then had to express that in my body. I walked around the large studio, and she called out each of their names at random; I had to "become" that character instantly and walk as they would. I came to know each of my four ancestors from the inside out.

Several other friends helped by reading the script and coaching me in French Canadian idioms and accents. This project was taking me way outside my comfort zone, so I was very grateful for their help.

My dancer friend's gift of her time was especially generous since we were meeting in the last few weeks before she moved out west. Before she left, she gave me the name and number of a Halifax director she thought might agree to work with me, Leanna Todd. Leanna and I brought *To Be Métis: One Woman's Journey* to the stage as part of the 2003 Halifax Fringe Festival.

In the play, there is a crucial supporting role. A rattle was shaken to mark each time I transitioned between the four characters and myself. It was essential to mark the transitions, because there were only slight costume and set changes, which happened onstage in front of the audience. I make these changes as myself, the storyteller, talking to the audience while doing so to provide them with parts of the story that linked each character. At each sounding of the rattle, I either became the character I was about to portray or returned to being myself.

In ceremony, the rattle is used to call in the ancestors, so it was perfect for what I was doing. I smudged before each performance, because I realized that I was calling in my family members, and their spirits were coming to help me tell their stories. Doing the play was not ceremony, but I was honouring my people in a way that was sacred. A dear friend took on the role of shaking the rattle for all the performances throughout the festival.

We did ten performances that week. Initially, the audiences were small, then word about the play spread, and I got an excellent review in the Halifax paper. At the last show, there was standing room only, and I received a raucous standing ovation at the end. My heart was in my throat as I called Leanna up from the audience and my friend from backstage to share the credit for this theatrical adventure.

For a few years, the play found its way onto more stages in Nova Scotia and Manitoba. By far the most memorable staging was a performance my oldest sister organized in Winnipeg. She invited several Métis community leaders, including Yvon Dumont, former lieutenant-governor of Manitoba, and J. Gabriel Dufault, then president of the Union Nationale Métisse Saint-Joseph du Manitoba, the oldest Métis organization in the country. My sister put up posters throughout the North End, so a number of other members of the Métis community came as well.

The presence of so many Métis community leaders was humbling as well as an honour, but that was not what made the evening so memorable. This was the first time that members of both my birth and adoptive families would meet. I was glad of this, but I also knew it would be emotional for me and that I wouldn't be able to stay grounded and focused if I interacted with any of them before the show. My warrior sister was my protector, standing guard as I prepared in a room off to the side of the hall the audience was gathering in so I could get ready in privacy. I heard an exchange between her and someone on the other side of the door that made me chuckle. My brother Rob, from my adoptive family—whom I hadn't yet seen on that trip—was looking for me. My sister, known for her no-nonsense directness, refused to let him in. Not knowing who she was, he explained to her that he was my brother. My sister went toe to toe with him, saying, "And I'm her sister." I shake my head as I write this, many years later; my life is full of these strange, mind-bending, heart-melting moments. Because of who Rob and I were to each other, as well as the vulnerability that was always present in him, I opened the door a crack to soften the blow and whispered a quick, "Hello, glad you're here, talk with you after." Then I returned to my preparations.

Another moment from that evening that I will always treasure was a comment my auntie Pat made afterward. I had been extra nervous about this performance, not only while telling the story, which encompassed significant parts of the history of my Nation, to many people who knew our history much better than I did, but also because I had the audacity to be acting the part of my grandmother, whom I had never met, in front of two of her daughters! The audience was stacked with people who would know whether or not I'd gotten my ancestors and the story right. I felt the pressure.

After the show, Auntie Pat's first words to me were, "Well, you sure are your grandmother's granddaughter!"

Apparently, my portrayal of her had been spot on. *Maarsii, Grand-Mère.*

# Interlude

# ELZÉAR GOULET

Took a trip to Winnipeg in the month of May
I wanted to walk where you ran that day
I found the old hotel on a street we both know well
And I walked in your footsteps
I walked your way

Right down to the river, or so the story goes
Kicked off my shoes, felt the mud between my toes
A light breeze was stirring in the warm spring air
And I offered tobacco there

While I watched the brown leaves float and flow beyond my sight
I prayed that you would help me tell our story that night
To honour your spirit is all I want to do
Because I owe so much of who I am to you

You really did your part back then in the days of Riel
To keep our Nation strong, oh so many great ones fell
And I want to walk my own path, head held high and unafraid
To honour the choices that you made

I lingered by the river, oh, I didn't want to leave
It took so long to find you, and my heart still needs to grieve
But the Métis Nation needs us today, as it did then
And the path you cleared with courage calls again

You've shone a light, Grandfather, on this life that I live
So I'll walk back up to the here and now and see what I can give
And I hope when I meet you someday in the Spirit World
You will recognize this Métis girl
Oh, you will recognize this Métis girl

IV

# CULTURAL BLINDNESS

Pelicans are synchronized swimmers. They glide by in a *V* with its open end forward, the broad white bowls of their bodies stabilizing their curving necks, their long slender beaks equipped with a light-orange pouch underneath. I loved sitting on the dock at the family cottage, watching as their webbed feet propelled them forward in the grey-green water of Netley Creek at exactly the same pace as each other, five or seven of them swimming as one. Poetry in motion.

Collaboration is their nature. They follow schools of fish, enclosing them and narrowing the opening until the moment they all plunge in their beaks and feed. A shared harvest. Oneness expressed in the practical necessities of everyday life.

They make kinship look so easy. And beautiful.

I had come to the cottage at Netley for a few days after a week in Baltimore, taking a course called Indigenous Social Determinants of Health. Having received a fellowship in a three-year program of study for Indigenous health practitioners, starting in 2007, each summer I was flown to different locations on Turtle Island to gather with Indigenous colleagues from Canada, the US, Australia, New Zealand, Mexico, and Nicaragua, for one week. My cohort and teachers were an amazing array of leaders in Indigenous health. Among them were trailblazers from many Indigenous nations in Canada and the US, Maori knowledge carriers and front-line workers, community-based primary health care workers from rural and remote places in Central America. Even the president of the Australian Indigenous Doctors' Association attended. Their collective wisdom was powerful. Being together gave us a direct experience of our shared reality; the different contexts we were working in were globally connected. Indigenous Peoples all over the world are healing from colonization.

We swam in synchrony for one week each summer—first in Baltimore, Maryland, then in Banff, Alberta, then in New York City—immersed in a sea of traditional and western knowledge, collectively generating and harvesting the wisdom that fed our souls and our professional practices. We spent most of our time in each other's company; we learned as a family. Subsequent summers, we greeted each other with the joy of kin reconnecting after not having seen each other for a while.

After my week in Baltimore, I flew to Winnipeg to visit my families, but first I headed straight to the cottage for the first few days to work on a paper I had to complete as a course requirement. I had a few days alone there to write, then Uncle Derry and Aunt Charlene came out and hosted a dinner, a kind gesture that allowed me to see a lot of Currie family relatives at once.

I watched my cousins' children race to see who would be the first one on the tire swing, just like we had when we were their age. Uncle Derry was a gracious host. There were fourteen of us in total, and the meal was a sit-down dinner, with every table in the place lined up end to end, stretching from the windows facing the water almost all the way to the back wall. The conversation was lively. I was quiet.

My heart was in my community of We'koqma'q, which I was writing about; my thoughts were with my Indigenous health colleagues. I had been writing for days about all the factors that contributed to the disproportionately high rates of physical and mental illness in our communities. My body was at the table, but my spirit was with my people. I realized then that this family didn't really know me anymore—with the exception of Uncle Derry and Aunt Charlene. Those two had made a point of accompanying me on this wild path of rediscovery, because they wanted to support me but also because they wanted to learn themselves. It wasn't that my other relatives were unkind. I looked around at these good people whom I had known through my growing-up years and felt a profound disconnect. I realized that my reality, Indigenous reality, the Métis and Mi'kmaw communities I was part of, and the international community of Indigenous health practitioners were just beyond the scope of my Currie family's knowledge.

"Why were you in Baltimore, Andrea?" my cousin asked.

"I was part of a group of Indigenous Peoples from around the world taking a course on Indigenous social determinants of health," I replied, grateful to be asked.

"Well, that sounds interesting. Was that your first time in Baltimore? What did you think of the city?"

My words dissolved in my throat. I was ready to describe the learning community we had created, eager to share the insights I had gained. My family seemed more interested in whether or not I had done any sightseeing.

This cousin just didn't know what they didn't know, so they had no questions to ask. Years earlier, they were happy to hear that I had reconnected with my birth family, but once they had expressed that, the conversation had been over. Sitting next to them at the table, elbow to elbow, I felt very far away.

I was raised to be polite. I carried myself well that evening, showing genuine interest in what was going on in their lives, laughing and carrying on. But I felt invisible. I had to put back on the same costume I had worn for the first seventeen years of my life to try to fit in. I looked like the same person they had always known. The fact that I had never really been that person was lost on them; that was the only version of me they knew, the only version they could relate to. Despite being surrounded by people whom I was expected to relate to as family, I felt invisible and lonely.

The next day, Uncle Derry and I were talking. He asked me if I had enjoyed the family gathering. Our relationship has always been strong enough to hold honesty and complexity, so I told him the truth: it was good to see everyone and hear how they were doing, but I didn't feel at home among them anymore. I was different now in ways that my adoptive family could not see. It wasn't that they didn't want to; it was just that growing up in and being part of the dominant culture had left them with only their own reference points for understanding their own reality and the realities of others.

This has a name: cultural blindness.

According to the American Psychology Association's *Dictionary of Psychology*, cultural blindness is "the inability to understand how particular matters might be viewed by people of a different culture because of a rigid adherence to the views, attitudes, and values of one's own culture or because the perspective of one's own culture is sufficiently limiting to make it difficult to see alternatives."[32]

Uncle Derry was compassionate. He went further in his effort to understand, asking me what was most powerful for me in the process of reclaiming my Métis identity. He commented on the relationships I had created with members of my birth family, recognizing how this must have been very healing for me. I told him that yes, reconnecting with my mother, my siblings, my extended Métis family had been profound, so much so that I would never be able to find adequate words to describe it, but that was not the *most* powerful part of the experience. I told him that most powerful for me was reconnecting with my culture.

The look on his face showed bafflement. He thought for a few seconds, then said, "Really! Imagine culture being more important than family."

A light bulb came on in my mind in that instant. In its glare, I saw cultural blindness. How one of the most intelligent, compassionate, well-informed, socially conscious people I have ever met could not grasp that culture could be more important than family to anyone, to me. I saw how hard it can be for settler people to really understand how culture is our lifeblood, how it shapes us and holds us, teaches and guides us, heals and supports and comforts us, because their culture permeates our collective life so thoroughly that they never even have to think about it—to the point that they are not even aware of how steeped they are in their own culture, nor of how embedded it is in the structure of every institution and how most of society reinforces and perpetuates its dominance so it is always there for them.

How can a person whose culture has been dominant for centuries without continuous attempts to attack it, eradicate it, denigrate it, and assimilate it into another culture, without its being despised and reduced to a fraction of its former self, truly understand the deep value of culture?

Those of us who have had our cultures ripped from us, beaten out of us, who have heard hateful things said about our cultures throughout the centuries since contact with the Europeans, who have watched our languages dwindle to rare whispers, who have watched the lands and waters that are part of us be exploited and ruined, who have had to fight to save what's left of our cultures and revitalize as much of what has been lost as we can … we know how important culture is.

If you want to understand the importance of culture, try to imagine living without yours, if you can.

What would you have lost?

Who would you be?

# A GREAT HONOUR ON A HEALER'S PATH

I heard the heavy door of the community hall swing open on its rusty hinges. I looked up from setting plates of food on the snack table to see who had arrived. It was one of our residential school survivors. It was the fall of 2003, and my co-workers and I were hosting a meeting for them. Nora Bernard, the Mi'kmaw woman who blazed the trail toward recognition and compensation for survivors, was coming to We'koqma'q to organize survivors to demand compensation for the harms suffered at the Shubenacadie Indian Residential School.

The man who had just come in took a quick look around and saw a few other survivors sitting at the long tables, sipping tea from disposable cups. I met his eyes, dark pools of hurt. Before any of us could even say hello, he turned on his heel and left without so much as a word, the door clanging shut behind him.

At that time, for many in our We'koqma'q Residential School Survivors group, just being in a room with other survivors was too much.

That was the beginning of what has now added up to two decades of shared pain, immeasurable healing and growth, epic resilience, and more laughter than anyone ever expected. Years of being honoured by the trust of this group of Elders, accompanying them on a journey from not being able to handle even being in a room together to becoming a family full of love and mutual support. How do I tell this story?

They would tell me to start with Nora.

By the time Nora Bernard arrived at the meeting in We'koqma'q that day, she had been working on the issue of compensation for residential school survivors in Canada for a couple of years. The first thing she had to do was to convince a Halifax lawyer to take the case and get the class action lawsuit certified. The certification of this and several similar lawsuits representing survivors across the country resulted in the federal government signing the Indian Residential Schools Settlement Agreement in 2006. Nora's courage and determination in her quest for justice for residential school survivors—travelling to communities, meeting with survivors in community halls like ours, educating lawyers, tirelessly lobbying until the federal government had to listen—will never be forgotten by those she fought for.

Nora's visit and her campaign were the reason that survivors in We'koqma'q got together. From there, they formed an ongoing group. Those first meetings were tense; the pain that the survivors had carried for so many years leaked out in intolerance and anger. "We were so mad back then," they say to me when we reminisce about those early days. Yet they kept on coming. Why? Because gathering and being together is a time-honoured way for Indigenous Peoples to heal, and it was good to be with people who knew what they had been through without them having to explain. Their need for the company of others who understood must have been very strong, because it won out over their initial reactivity and awkward silences.

There were larger gatherings too. Several took place in Unama'ki; most of the We'koqma'q survivors attended these along with survivors from other communities. Again, though, there were times when just walking through the door would overwhelm some of them, and tears and anger would erupt, making it too painful for them to stay. The others saw this lashing out for what it was and were compassionate, accepting that not everyone is ready to heal at the same time. It takes the time it takes. We learned that together.

Communicating with survivors about meetings and conferences led to our setting up monthly meetings. They wanted to get together on a regular basis.

And so the We'koqma'q Residential School Survivors group was born. It would grow to be a force in the community, bringing healing to survivors, their descendants, and the community as a whole. The community healing aspect is so important. Everyone in our communities has been impacted by residential schools through the now well-documented intergenerational effects of the schools on families and communities. The depth of shared grief over the loss of so many children wreaked havoc with social cohesion, bringing about the lateral violence that is a logical consequence of lacking the power and resources to fight the real enemy. Because the wounding was collective, so too is the healing.

Once the survivors had created and held space for each other to heal and reconnect with themselves and each other, core teachings about generosity and sharing surfaced in a natural inclination to find ways to include the community, especially children, in the healing process. They initiated project after project that had a broader reach than the group members themselves, watched their efforts ripple out to touch others, and felt love and gratitude flow back to them in return.


## THE EXHIBIT

During my 1998 trip to Winnipeg, my birth mother took me to the office of the Manitoba Métis Federation to get me registered as a member of the Métis Nation. While waiting in the reception area, I saw three poster-size plaques on the wall. Each had a black-and-white photo of a prominent Elder in the Métis community, under which was printed a brief biographical profile. One of them was my grandmother. Seeing her looking out at me that day and reading a synopsis of her life gave me more of a sense of belonging than the laminated status card, still warm in my hand, ever could.

As I came to know our We'koqma'q survivors better, I was struck by how each of them had accomplished so much in spite of the trauma they had experienced at the Shubenacadie Indian Residential School. I pitched to them the idea of creating a series of plaques, one to honour each of them, that could be displayed as a permanent exhibit in our We'koqma'q Mi'kmawey School. They loved the idea. We obtained funding from the United Church of Canada, hired someone to help me, and set to work. For the better part of 2011, we interviewed each survivor—but not about the abuses they suffered at the school. Instead, we focused on what they had accomplished in their lives. Their resilience manifested in so many ways. One had become a social worker and another a nurse. One was well known for his trapping skills, which he taught to the youth. Another was a wild game butcher. One had been a band councillor; another was the Kji Saqamaw, Grand Chief of the entire Mi'kmaw Nation. One had become the main Mi'kmaw language teacher at our school, and also represented the east on several national boards working on issues affecting survivors across the country. Another made and sold beadwork to many pleased customers. One became a teacher, and after getting her master's degree, worked with other Mi'kmaw leaders on the development and implementation of Mi'kmaw Kina'matmewey, the Mi'kmaw education authority created to bring self-determination into the education of our children. Another was a textile artist who created beautiful traditional regalia. One was a professional cook who had worked in several restaurants.

We got a We'koqma'q community member who was a photographer to take photos for the plaques, and we worked at editing and condensing the story of each person so it would fit into the available space. The survivors gave us their final approval before we sent their photographs and biographical profiles to the company that was making the plaques for us.

At the same time, we decided to avail ourselves of some of the funding that was flowing through the Truth and Reconciliation Commission's commemoration fund and design a monument to honour everyone from We'koqma'q who had attended the Shubenacadie Indian Residential School.

## THE MONUMENT

The entire group reviewed different sizes and shapes of monuments and together chose a basic structure. On a whiteboard in the community room of the health centre, we created the design. After several meetings, the design was finalized, and we invited the owner of a local monument company to attend one of our meetings so the survivors could explain what they wanted.

The monument man respectfully listened to several group members as they described the monument they wanted, which would be composed of three black granite columns—the centre one about five feet tall and the two flanking columns each about four feet tall—all standing on a grey granite foundation. They explained in more detail what they wanted on the monument and why.

"On each of the two side columns, we want the Mi'kmaw hieroglyphic symbols for *girl* and for *boy*," stated then Grand Chief Ben Sylliboy, "to symbolize the separation of girls and boys in the school, how we weren't even allowed to see our sisters and brothers."

There would be a quote from Nora Bernard on one of the columns, and for the other, Magit Poulette requested a quote from the poem "I Lost My Talk" by her dear friend, Mi'kmaw poet Rita Joe, a survivor of Shubenacadie who was originally from We'koqma'q:

I lost my talk.
The talk you took away.
Let me find my talk
So I can teach you about me.[33]

"Justice," Nora said in a 2007 interview. "I wanted justice for my First Nations people that attended the residential schools—not only down here—throughout Canada."[34]

On the central column, the name of every person from We'koqma'q who had gone to the Shubenacadie Indian Residential School would be etched, with crosses or feathers next to the names of those who had crossed over to Spirit. One of the survivors explained that it would be up to the families of the survivors who had passed to choose which symbol best honoured the spirituality of their loved one. In the very centre, there would also be a traditional Mi'kmaw eight-pointed star in a circle, with each quadrant painted one of the four sacred colours: red, yellow, black, and white.

At the base of the monument would be written *We'koqma'q Residential School Survivors*, and at the top, *Ma'tlipia'tiwkw App*. One of the group members translated this for the monument man. "It means, 'It will never happen again.'"

With the presentation of the design complete, there was a discussion of the price. It was going to be costly, but we had the funds in our budget. One of the survivors, who could never pass on the opportunity to sweeten a deal, suggested that since we were spending thousands of dollars, perhaps our friend from the monument company could throw in a bench for people to sit on as they contemplated all of it. The monument man, with an expression on his face that was a mix of amusement and respect for the survivor's business acumen, agreed. So, there is a lovely semicircular stone bench in front of the monument for visitors to sit on. We call it "Cecil's Bench."

## THE GRAND OPENING

In December of 2012, we held the grand opening of the exhibit *Honouring Our We'koqma'q Residential School Survivors—Past and Present* and an unveiling of the monument, which was installed in front of the school in our community. Our guest of honour was Justice Murray Sinclair, chair of the Truth and Reconciliation Commission. Our Chief and Band Councillors, flanked by our MP and our MLA, watched as the survivors arrived in a procession, accompanied by a drum group made up of their children and grandchildren, singing the Mi'kmaw Honour Song. The eldest survivor in our group and the Grand Chief lifted the purple-satin cloth covering the monument and revealed the beautiful, powerful stonework—a precise execution of the survivors' complex design. There were cheers and applause from the crowd. The whole community was in attendance that day.

We all went into the school, where the survivors escorted people through the exhibit. Children and grandchildren of survivors stood proudly beside the plaques of their family members, taking pictures to mark the occasion. A feast was held in the school gym, with young children from our community school singing in Mi'kmaw and then going out into the crowd to present each of the survivors with a toy: dolls for the women and toy soldiers for the men. The children had learned that these Elders had not been allowed to have toys at residential school, and they wanted to do something about that. Murray Sinclair gave a moving speech, honouring our survivors and commending them and the whole community for the healing work we were doing together. Everywhere you looked, people were smiling from ear to ear. The next day, our MP, who had flown to Ottawa a few hours after the event, stood up in the

House of Commons and gave the We'koqma'q residential school survivors national recognition for their accomplishments.

The survivors didn't stop there. They decided there should be a curriculum guide to accompany the exhibit and the monument. So, together, we wrote and produced a couple hundred copies of a curriculum guide and delivered it to the We'koqma'q Mi'kmawey School. Eventually they grew concerned that the booklets would just sit on a shelf and not get used, so they requested a meeting with the director of education and a couple of teachers who were also descendants of survivors. At that meeting, the school staff requested the development of a one-hour workshop that could be delivered in the time frame of a high school class. We developed the workshop, wrote a workshop guide, and produced multiple copies of it. Then the survivors acknowledged that they needed training in delivering the workshop and asked me to organize a public-speaking course for them. Two trainers came from the local Christopher Leadership Course organization to meet with the survivors and discuss their needs. They agreed to design a public-speaking training program with the specific objective of preparing the survivors to present the workshop. They also agreed to come to the community and deliver the training there to make it easier for everyone to attend. The trainers were visibly moved when they heard what the survivors had to say. Since acquiring public-speaking skills, the survivors have offered the workshop many times, presenting it to school classes, church and community groups, conferences, and our municipal councillors and staff.

As the facilitator and therapist for the group, I have seen every person who has come in contact with the We'koqma'q residential school survivors be touched by their stories, their dignity, their clarity of purpose, and their determination to heal themselves and educate others so that no more children will suffer the way they did—from the woman at the photography shop who laid out the plaques to the technician who made them, from the owner of the monument company to the two public-speaking trainers, from the numerous reporters to all our local politicians. The We'koqma'q residential school survivors have found a place in the hearts of everyone who meets them.

And they're still at it. A couple of years ago, one of the survivors decided that children finishing their kindergarten year in our school should have traditional regalia for their graduation ceremony. At that age, the survivors' own clothing had been taken away and burned, and they had been forced to wear uniforms that were strange and uncomfortable to them. She wanted the little ones to have ribbon skirts and ribbon vests to wear, so she got some other Elders to help her make regalia. When the children put the skirts and vests on, they danced around. The teacher decided that she should wear regalia too, so she had a skirt made. Then all the teachers in the school wanted their own regalia. A CBC reporter came to write a story about this, which was posted online.[35] She had so much material, she ended up also making a half-hour radio documentary.[36] It has aired a number of times on regional broadcasts.

As I write this, the entire country is reeling from the discovery of thousands of unmarked graves of children at the sites of residential schools across the land. The number of graves of children who died alone, without their loved ones, is now over eleven thousand and will continue to grow, as only a fraction of the schools' grounds has been investigated so far. Though our group members already knew that children died at the schools, this has triggered upsetting memories for them. One has decided she can no longer go to church. Several others find themselves crying at random moments of the day. Another has felt the same fear she felt while a little girl at Shubenacadie, realizing now that she could have ended up in one of those unmarked graves.

A young musician here in Mi'kma'ki, DeeDee Austin, whose great-grandmother was a residential school survivor, recently wrote and released a song called "Buried Truth" about what happened to the students at the schools and how the truth that was buried for so long is finally being revealed. After I shared a recording of the song with the survivors and saw how grateful they were that a teenage singer-songwriter was speaking up for them, I contacted DeeDee to ask her to come to their annual summer barbecue and surprise them with a live performance.

Her song lyrics pull no punches:

They scrubbed our skin with a wire brush
They broke the boundaries of all trust[37]

The survivors listened to the harsh lyrics and touching music with respect and appreciation for our young guest. Afterward, their shining smiles expressed the hope that comes from being seen and heard and cared about. And DeeDee, who felt honoured to be invited to sing for them, was showered with love and hugs.

●●●

Once again, a local reporter was there to capture the moment and carry the story further. The healing energy ripples out from the We'koqma'q Residential School Survivors group to anyone whose heart and spirit are open and ready.

I get in trouble sometimes. Biological and adoptive relatives leave me voice mails, and it takes me a long time to return their calls. Sometimes I completely forget. Or archive the message so many times that it gets lost in a long queue of calls to be returned. I wonder about this. I don't intend to hurt anyone, so why do I do this sometimes? It's not that I don't care. Is it the behaviour of someone who has become desensitized to the importance of family relationships? Whatever it is, I am not proud of it, and I take full responsibility.

How can I explain to people whose experience of family is being bonded to their parents, siblings, or cousins because they grew up together in a shared experience that it is not like that for me? That the only person who really shared my experience of family before I left home was my younger brother, Rob, and he was returned to the Children's Aid Society like an unwanted item. And then he died too young. As a result, I've come to define family very differently from how a lot of other people do.

Most of my family members are extraordinary human beings who are related to me because of the relationships we created. Some of them have the other kind of family too, as well as the less conventional bond between us. These are the people I share my life with on the regular, who hold me steady when that is what I need and turn to me to hold them steady when that is what they need. I didn't have this support growing up, and it is a miracle for which I never cease to be grateful. My sense of security is rooted in this wondrous web of connections. I am so loved.

In my adoptive family, my uncle Derry has been a constant, and my older brother and I have grown closer as the years have passed. With most of my siblings in my birth family, the deep love we feel for each other does not require reinforcement through frequent communication, and I get the feeling that none of us are very good at that. We've all walked our separate rocky roads when it comes to family. I have an unspoken agreement with most of them that we will not set each other up with expectations or obligations. When we do connect, it is pure love and pleasure.

I once heard a well-known writer talk about his siblings and how he thinks about those relationships a lot because "they go through your whole life with you." I had to parse the meaning of this, because it didn't sit right with me. Out of the siblings I grew up with, Rob was closer to me than anyone until he died, but my older adoptive brother and I weren't close at all until well into our adult years. On a recent visit to spend time with him, I found out that this was due to our adoptive mother's manipulation and control of the family narrative; she wanted Rob and me to believe that we were nothing like our older brother, the golden child who could do no wrong. Now in our sixties, my older brother and I have only just discovered how this was not true, though it shaped our relationship back then. What that writer said rings at least somewhat true with my birth siblings, although we didn't meet until I was in my late thirties: in a way, they have been with me through my whole life, existing in separate but parallel worlds. Even before we knew each other, we shared experiences of disconnection and loss, resilience and reconnection, that make us kin just as much as time spent together does for other people.

My relationship with Maman was another thing altogether, and one particular family visit with her sticks in my heart like a thorn.

She was the exception to the "no obligations" rule. Whenever I came to Winnipeg, she wanted more of my time than I was able to give. I get that we had missed many years. I will never have enough time with any members of my birth family. I am certain that when I leave this world, I will still feel like I'm trying to catch up with each of them. Those of my siblings that I'm close to also feel this, but we're pragmatic people. We do the best we can and carry that feeling with grace. It's just part of the perpetual grief we live with, an underground stream murmuring, a subwoofer that produces more of a feeling than a sound.

But Maman's lifetime of living in denial about her less-than-stellar years as a parent afforded her a sense of entitlement that I found baffling.

My son was with me on that particular trip. We were dividing our time between both families, some childhood friends, and some Elders and new friends in the Métis community we were getting to know. It was tricky, but I did my best to be fair and diplomatic. I hope that someday I can sit down and talk with other Sixties Scoop survivors about how they cope with this challenge. It's quite the flow chart, a messy map of our hearts.

No amount of time we spent with Maman was enough for her. My mother, a beautiful, dignified woman in so many ways and a respected Elder in the Métis community at that point in her life, would pout when we left her house to go elsewhere. Hoping to ease her unhappiness, I made a few calls and rejigged our plans, enabling my son and me to spend the Saturday afternoon with her before we flew back to Nova Scotia. I explained to him that his grandmother wanted more time with us before we left for home.

We were greeted warmly and settled in for our visit. But both of us were taken aback when Maman started preparing to go out. If she were going somewhere that a child could go, we would have gone with her, but she was going to the bar. She didn't want to miss playing darts.

My son was confused. That's why this memory is hard: my child's feelings were hurt. I tried to explain to him that it wasn't that he was not important to his grandmother. What we were experiencing was part of something bigger than us: the reality of being part of a family busted up by the Sixties Scoop. Like with me and my unreturned phone calls, prioritizing family didn't come naturally to her.

We watched TV. When she wasn't home by suppertime, we left.

# TO THE ONE WHO WAS MY GATEWAY

funny I never dreamed of you
our severing so absolute
nothing left to grow a dream from

steeped in solitude
emptiness for miles
aloneness a buffer
that no disappointment could breach

we met
there was sweetness
no longer natural
the first sharp jolt of candy
that fades quickly on the tongue

(the longing that had driven us
was nearly out of gas)

your statement:
I don't call my children, my children call me
echoed across a canyon thirty-eight years wide

your flaws the heartache of murky glass
your imperfections generous permission
to be unapologetically myself

the real gift you gave me
revealed itself slowly
its contours gradually coming into view
rising up from somewhere
below the horizon

my culture
my community
my people
stepped out of the half-light
greeting my innermost self
quaffing a ghostly thirst

we had some years
I called you Maman out of respect
honouring our awkward truth

what I really loved you for
still deeply love you for
with gratitude that can span any canyon is
how you gave me back to myself

you gave me life twice

# HOW OLD AM I NOW?

A memory from childhood: the Manitoba sun hot on my dark hair. A lot has happened since I was a child here. This time, I'm back for the Truth and Reconciliation (TRC) hearings in Winnipeg, one of seven national events held throughout the country between 2010 and 2014 to allow people to hear and honour residential school survivors' stories, as well as to enter these into the historical record of this country so that everyone knows about the history and legacy of the residential school system—better late than never. This is an important step in the process of decolonization. As my teacher and friend, Elder Albert Marshall from Eskasoni First Nation, reminds us, a relationship is founded on the exchange of stories. When we can hear each other's stories, we can build new relationships.

But it is hard for survivors to tell their stories, and it is hard for family members to hear them. Truly, it is hard for anyone to hear them. So at each TRC national event, there are about fifty healers and mental health professionals spread throughout the gathering, available for immediate emotional support: inside the main room, where survivors are telling the commissioners their stories and having them recorded; in a room where films are being screened; in the lobby and coffee areas; and outside, at the Sacred Fire.

That's where I am, feeling the heat of the sun on my head.

Some of the survivors come here with the same damp tissues they cried into when they were giving their testimony. They make an offering of their sacred waters at the Sacred Fire, placing the tissues in its cleansing flames. Some are very quiet. Some wail in a way that goes right through you. It's an honour to be here to support them, to bear witness to their pain and their resilience, their fierce reclamation of themselves.

Different members of my family and some friends come by. They come to attend the event and to hang out with me when I'm not working. I introduce my brother Rob to Elder Albert, who also made the trip from Unama'ki. To make this introduction connecting loved ones means more to me than to either of them; they humour me. My nephew is there, my oldest sister's son. I see a couple of old friends from the first seventeen years of my life, and I'm glad they're attending the event. And then there's the day Uncle Derry comes.

He's going to meet me at the Sacred Fire circle, where prayers and ceremony begin each day. Finding each other turns out to be pretty challenging. People are thronging six or seven deep at the top of the circle on the grass; all the seats in the circular stone amphitheatre below are already taken. I manage to snag a spot down below in the first row for the two of us. I scan the crowd, hoping to spot him. I see him, but he doesn't see me. I ask the person sitting next to me to save my spot and take off after him. I bound up the closest set of stone steps, catch up with him, give him a quick hug and kiss, then grab his hand to lead us back to our seats down in front. It's so packed that I have to hold on to his hand as we weave our way through the crowd so we don't get separated. We get to our seats just as the ceremony begins. We sit there through a couple of prayers, my hand still cradled in the softness of his seventy-six-year-old hand. In this moment, I feel this simple physical gesture expressing so much that is indescribable. How being seen by him throughout my life has been a source of protection, a safe place. How I have been holding this hand—and only this hand—for as long as I can remember, since I was a very little girl, right through all the changes in my life, and I'm still holding it at this moment, right where I'm supposed to be, helping my people heal here on the banks of the river where my ancestors made camp centuries ago. This hand has been holding me steady for many years.

Salty streams of gratitude wet my face.

In my mind, the question "How old am I now?"

# HOW TO UNRAVEL A LIFE

**1. Start with a life that is already tenuous and starting
to come apart.**

Rob had been slowly spiralling into poverty and isolation. His marriage
had broken up—the end of the happiest years of his life. His daughter
left with her mom, and his son stayed with him in the family home,
attending high school and living on his own part of the time, while Rob
was away on the road as a long-haul truck driver. The many phone calls
Rob made to his son from the truck and stocking the freezer at home
with frozen pizzas sustained this arrangement for a while, until, as one
might expect, my nephew decided he needed family around on a daily
basis and went to live with his mom.

While parked on the side of the road during a winter blizzard with
whiteout conditions, Rob's truck was rear-ended by a snowplow whose
driver couldn't see the pylons behind the truck that indicated that Rob
was stopped there. However, Rob was found at fault for this accident,
resulting in the loss of his job and making it hard for him to get another
one in the small world of transport companies in Winnipeg. When the
house was sold in the divorce settlement, he used that money for rent
and bills until it ran out and he needed a cheaper place to live. Always
a big guy, Rob went back to working as a bouncer, something he had
done as a much younger man. The bar he worked at was in a seedy hotel
in a not-so-great part of town, and part of his pay was a room down
the hall. Now his housing was linked to his employment, not the most
stable of situations.

## 2. Add a lack of good health care.

Unresolved trauma from childhood abuse combined with his tumultuous adolescence left Rob without some of the life skills needed to do well on his own. For instance, he had no idea how important it is to have a family doctor and regular checkups. There were no health care providers in Rob's life who knew him and had an understanding of what his baseline wellness was and could therefore see changes occurring over time. Rob had raging psoriasis that was never treated with any consistency. I always felt that the eruptions on his skin looked angry, like years' worth of suppressed rage literally bubbling up and making its way out of him the only way it could.

For Rob, there were no regular checkups; he was too focused on daily survival to give much thought to his health care. When he started getting abdominal pain in the summer of 2011, he tried to soldier through it. When it became unbearable, he did what most of us do when we have no doctor to call for an appointment: he went to the emergency room of the closest hospital. Based only on Rob's report of the severe pain he was experiencing and bloodwork that showed an elevated white blood cell count, he was diagnosed with an abdominal infection, prescribed antibiotics, and sent home. No tests were ordered that could have provided more accurate information about what was going on. Why did no one flag the possibility of colon cancer at that time?

One of the most common forms of discrimination that Indigenous people face in the health care system, especially when we present in the emergency departments of our local hospitals, is the racist assumption that when we say we are experiencing pain, we are faking it in order to obtain painkillers, for ourselves or to sell to others. This prejudice has been reported by many health care providers when anonymously surveyed, as well as by Indigenous patients who did not receive the attention and care they badly needed. Was Rob, with his dark complexion, hair, and eyes, recognized as Indigenous by the doctor on duty that day and dismissed as just one more drug-seeking Indian?

On one of my trips to Winnipeg in the year that followed, I took a break from visiting Rob in the hospital and went to the main library in downtown Winnipeg. Libraries have always been a source of solace for me. I sat by a bright window in a comfy chair and picked up a magazine, hoping for some light reading. Instead, I found myself reading about the prevalence of misdiagnoses in the health care system. I learned that doctors will most often go to the most common causes of the symptoms a patient is presenting with, and many serious illnesses are missed in initial consults due to this line of thinking. The advice to patients is to always ask if anything besides the health care provider's initial diagnosis could be causing their symptoms. As health care consumers, very few of us are skilled in advocating for this quality of care. Rob certainly wasn't.

Even if he hadn't been discriminated against in the emergency room—and it would not be a stretch to think that he was—he did not receive a thoughtful and thorough assessment of his condition.

Rob had told me about his "abdominal infection" on a phone call that summer as we made plans for his first trip to Unama'ki to visit me. I was planning to fly him out on my frequent flyer points as a gift for his fiftieth birthday. We were both excited. I recall Rob telling me that he had not been feeling all that great but that he was on antibiotics and was sure he'd be better in time to enjoy the trip.

### 3. Make sure the person is part of a dysfunctional family so there is no cohesive network of support.

Rob and I had not told our adoptive mother about the trip. Neither of us was in regular contact with her. She and our father had moved to BC years before, and she had stayed there after our dad died in 1998. Phone calls with her were few and far between.

The week before Rob was to fly to Nova Scotia, I came home to find a voice mail from our mother, just letting me know that she had called and asking me to call her back. No indication of anything urgent. I had decided it was time to tell her about Rob's upcoming trip, and I knew it would not be well received. She always felt that visiting her should be our number one priority, so I had to be prepared for an attempt to make me feel guilty. I put off calling her back until I was in the right frame of mind to handle a toxic conversation. She called on a Saturday;

I called her back the following Tuesday. We started off with the usual small talk. After several minutes of innocuous chat, I told her that Rob was coming to visit me. What she said next still burns in my memory. "Oh no, he won't be, dear. He's in the hospital."

Rob's abdominal pain had not gone away with the antibiotics, and he had ended up back in the emergency department on the previous Saturday. He was diagnosed with advanced colon cancer and told that he had to have surgery immediately. Like so many of us do when we feel ill, he called his mother. It must be hard-wired into us, this instinct, kicking in before rational thought can determine who would be the best person to call. Because in Rob's case, it sure wasn't her. Our mother had kept this news to herself.

A young boy lies in a hospital bed. He is frightened and in pain. Burns cover 40 percent of his small body. Someone has doused him with alcohol and then, unimaginably, has set him on fire.

He cries for his mother.

His mother has set him on fire.

It doesn't seem to matter what kind of mother a child has lost, or how perilous it may be to dwell in her presence. It doesn't matter whether she hurts or hugs. Separation from mother is worse than being in her arms when the bombs are exploding. Separation from mother is sometimes worse than being with her when she is the bomb.[38]

Not only had she failed to let me know she was calling about something urgent, our mother did not call our uncle Derry in Winnipeg, who should have been the first person she called. She left Rob to face life-threatening surgery all alone, without a family member there to support him, and to spend two more days dealing with the aftermath alone in the hospital. The intense fear and suffering Rob went through would have been eased by Uncle Derry's presence, had our mother cared enough about Rob to call and let him know.

As soon as I realized what she had done, I hung up the phone, called the hospital, and was put through to Rob's room. I fought back my tears.

"Rob! What happened? I just heard. I didn't know. I just talked to Mom."

"She didn't call you?"

"She left a message but didn't say it was urgent. I called her just now. I'm so sorry!"

"Bitch."

That was it. I knew right away we had to get Irene out of our heads. Dwelling on her cruelty was the last thing he needed at that moment. We had to focus on getting Rob the support he needed.

"Look, I'm going to hang up now and call Uncle Derry. I know he'll be there as soon as he can. I'll call you right back after I talk to him."

I called our uncle and told him what was going on. He was shocked. "Why didn't Irene call me?" asked my bewildered uncle. His naïveté is one of the things I love about him; in this case, it prevented him from seeing the reality of our adoptive mother's feelings about us, or the lack thereof.

"Can you go?" I asked.

He left for the hospital right away. I called Rob back and stayed on the line with him for the twenty minutes it took Uncle Derry to get to his bedside.

### 4. Stack the odds so that a medical misstep happens.

A few days later, Rob was sent home to his room in the hotel. Thanks to the basic human decency of the hotel manager, who knew Rob had no place to go, he was allowed to stay there even when he could not work for his lodging. A nurse was assigned to make home visits to check on his progress as he recovered. After a few days, it was obvious to her that Rob was not doing well. He felt sicker than he had in the hospital, post-op, and his colour was bad. When the nurse saw how ill he was, she told him to go back to the hospital right away.

Rob was septic. The reattachment of his colon after the cancerous part had been removed had not held. His abdominal cavity had filled with fecal matter, causing an infection so severe that it never went away. In the weeks and months that followed, Rob's health care team made a Herculean effort to heal the infection, pulling out the "big guns" in their arsenal of antibiotics—to no avail. Rob had that infection for the rest of his life. It prevented the incision from his surgery from ever healing, made it impossible for him to have chemo, and necessitated excruciatingly painful dressing changes that he had to endure several times a day.

He never went home again.

I called up the airline and explained that my brother would not be able to use his ticket and that under the circumstances, I wanted to use it to go and see him. The airline agreed.

That was the first of seven trips I made to Winnipeg that year.

During the first trip, there was a family meeting with the surgeon. I was there, as well as Uncle Derry, our adoptive mother, and a close family friend who was a nurse. Rob was present for most of it before he felt too ill to stay upright in the wheelchair and had to go back to his room. The doctor explained that the best-case scenario was Rob recovering from the infection so he would be eligible for chemotherapy. However, he was clear that there was no hope of Rob recovering from the cancer; it was too advanced by the time they had found it. Chemo would only buy him more time. The doctor cautioned us about the inexact science of prognosticating in cases like this and then estimated that Rob might have a year to live.

When I went to Rob's room after the meeting, he wanted to know what he had missed. I told him what the doctor had said but left out the prognosis. Rob asked me straight out how much time he had. It was the first of many times I had to be the bearer of bad news. I don't remember how I told him, but I remember his response: "If they're giving me a year, I'll take the year."

Rob died the following August, almost exactly one year from the date of the first botched surgery.

For me, that year was one of constantly feeling torn. I had a twelve-year-old son at home, in the tricky time between childhood and becoming a teenager. He was just starting his junior high years at the middle school he attended. He needed me there, and Rob needed me in Winnipeg. No matter where I was, I felt that I was letting someone down. If I had been asked at the start whether I was willing to go to Winnipeg seven times to support Rob, I would have been hard pressed to agree. I knew that my boy was at a delicate and challenging time in his life, and it was far from ideal for me to be away so much. He came with me on one trip in December. An acute care ward can be a scary and upsetting place for a kid. I will always be grateful to the friends and relatives who took him to the movies and other outings and gave him some fun times while I was with Rob.

In a recent conversation with my son, he told me about an essay he had written for a grade twelve English assignment about that time in our lives, entitled "The Year I Lived in My Best Friend's Basement." I feel like I really let him down. I wonder if he will be talking about this to a therapist someday.

Several of my trips were taken when it seemed the end of Rob's life was near. He had asked me to be there when he died, and I'd promised I would do my best. Time and again, he rallied and surprised us with what seemed like a bottomless well of resilience and will to live.

Uncle Derry went to the hospital every single day to keep Rob company. He only took days off when I was in town. Rob spent most of that year on the palliative care ward of St. Boniface Hospital, one of the longest resident stays there ever. When I was in Winnipeg, I moved right into his room, sleeping on a rollaway cot that I set up beside his bed at night and tucked away in his bathroom during the day. I took breaks to go for walks outside. One day, I ventured a bit farther on my outing and walked and window-shopped in Osborne Village, a funky neighbourhood in Winnipeg with great cafés, boutiques, and galleries. It was a cold winter day, and the snow under my boots made squeaking sounds. As I was walking, my phone rang. It was Rob, calling to ask when I was coming home.

# INDIGENOUS PAIN

The image of the stoic Indian is one of the most well-known stereotypes distorting how non-Indigenous people perceive us. One of the funniest scenes in the 1998 movie *Smoke Signals*[39] is when Adam Beach's character, Victor, instructs Evan Adams's character, Thomas, on how to be a stoic Indian. Victor tells Thomas that he has to stop smiling all the time and look mean, or white people will walk all over him. Thomas's attempts to modify his facial expressions accordingly are hilarious. Anishinaabe photographer Nadya Kwandibens has said, "There are no stoic Indians on my website."[40] Focusing on portraits of Indigenous Peoples in her work, Kwandibens shows us as smiling and laughing people so that the joys we experience are represented at least as frequently as the struggles.

The colonial lens through which many settler peoples see Indigenous Peoples has its roots in the early colonists' accounts of contact with the people they encountered when they arrived in what they myopically considered "uninhabited" territories. It seems clear when one reads these accounts that the colonists were too culture blind to consider the different ways people in different cultures express emotions, and they therefore projected the European concept of stoicism onto the original peoples of the lands they invaded. Stoicism has its roots in a school of thought founded in third-century Greece that emphasized virtue and living an ethical life, but the term has since evolved to mean the characteristic of being impervious to pain and/or repressing one's emotions. Since nothing in the colonizers' post-"Enlightenment" European rationalist education left room for the possibility of other ways of knowing, feeling, and expressing oneself, their perception of the stoicism of Indigenous Peoples was not questioned and solidified into a stereotype that still persists today.

Although there have been and continue to be efforts made to debunk the myth of Indigenous stoicism and to eliminate this stereotype, the racist belief persists, and the lack of understanding that flows from it is expressed in many settings that continue to harm us—the health care system being one of them.

A team of Indigenous and settler researchers in Mi'kma'ki engaged with a group of Mi'kmaw youth in an art-based project about their experiences of pain. They found that there was a theme of stoicism in the way their subjects related to their pain, but it was not this stereotype they were referencing. The young people explained their reasons for minimizing their pain and often not telling anyone about it. They talked about growing up with their parents and grandparents who had gone through a lot in their lives, and they didn't want to add to that.

All of the adults in their lives had been affected by the deeply disruptive centralization program of the Department of Indian Affairs in the 1940s, which forced Mi'kmaw families in all but two communities—Sipekne'katik (Shubenacadie) on the mainland and Eskasoni in Unama'ki (Cape Breton Island)—to move to one of those two reserves. In addition to this loss of connection to the land of their ancestors, many of these adults were also residential school survivors, or their descendants. The children were influenced by this in a number of ways. They spoke of not wanting to add to the pain they knew their parents and grandparents had already gone through. This sounds to me like empathy-driven self-censoring, which I suggest is different from stoicism.

Also, the residential school survivors had been forced to swallow their pain in order to survive—not just the pain inflicted upon them in the schools, but also the pain of coming home and feeling disconnected to their families and communities and true selves. This resulted in many survivors finding it very difficult to express emotions, so the children growing up around them got the tacit message that feelings were not something to be talked about. Centuries of profoundly painful attacks on Indigenous Peoples, our cultures, and our ways of life have led to resilience being highly valued, often twisted up into a teaching about the importance of being tough. It would be easy to see this through the lens of the stoicism trope, but I have experienced it in my work in Mi'kmaw communities more as an economy of emotion in response to potential overwhelm. People make choices, consciously and unconsciously, about which feelings to give space and attention to when facing a great deal to cope with.

One of the other things the children expressed in their artworks was that they made no distinction between physical and emotional pain. Pain is pain. In keeping with the Indigenous world view of wholeness and interconnectedness, they experienced their pain in a holistic way. As someone who has experienced both physical and emotional abuse, I have found that physical pain has been the easiest to heal from, while healing from emotional wounds is an ongoing and seemingly unending challenge. I wonder how many other survivors of cultural loss and emotional abuse would say the same. How does this impact the way we present physical pain when, in terms of dealing with the pain we experience, it is often the least of our worries?

Other research studies on the topic of how Indigenous people experience and express pain have found that the pervasiveness of misunderstanding around it is perpetuated by the lack of culturally appropriate training and tools for assessing our pain. When an Indigenous person presents to a health care provider and is asked about the pain they are experiencing, that patient's understanding of their pain is consciously or unconsciously—and to varying degrees—shaped by a world view in which health comprises a balance between the physical, mental, emotional, and spiritual aspects of the self, the family, the community, and the nation. When asked to choose a number between one and ten to describe the intensity of their pain, how are we supposed to make sense of that question? All of my pain or just some of it? My pain, or the pain of my family and community, which is also my pain?

Add to this the justifiable mistrust that the majority of Indigenous people have of settler health care providers, and you have a perfect storm of inadequate communication, flawed clinical conclusions, and very poor quality of care. If anyone needs to be convinced of this, there is the story of Joyce Echaquan, the thirty-seven-year-old Atikamekw mother of seven who died in a Quebec hospital in September 2020, minutes after begging for help from the nurses who were supposed to be caring for her. In the video she broadcast on Facebook less than an hour before she died, her agony is in shockingly stark contrast to the racist comments of the callous nurses. Indeed, Echaquan's story underscores the common belief held by many Indigenous individuals that it doesn't make any difference if we tell health care providers we are in pain, because they won't care anyway. That is not stoicism; that is a learned behaviour in which muting our pain becomes a coping mechanism.

There is also interesting work being done to generate knowledge about the impact of historical trauma on the neurobiology of pain. Not being a neurologist, my layperson's understanding is that many parts of the brain are involved in how we mediate our experiences of pain. The thalamus is one of them, and because it coordinates our sensory experience—what something feels like—with our conscious understanding of what we are experiencing, it involves our memories of not only physical pain but also social exclusion and loss. This early research connects pain with a person's social, emotional, and cultural experiences. Will this be another instance of empirical science eventually coming into alignment with Indigenous beliefs and teachings?

Asking "Grandma Google" for information on racism in the health care system yields a shamefully large number of results. At the end of the twenty-one pages is the statement, "In order to show you the most relevant results, we have omitted some entries very similar to the 205 already displayed." There is plenty of evidence out there that racism exists in health care, here and around the world.

One article reports findings from a study in which health care providers were asked about racism toward Indigenous patients that they had either witnessed or perpetrated themselves. The results were clear. "The stereotypes that care providers have about Indigenous people influence their clinical decision-making."[41] Several respondents acknowledged their assumptions that Indigenous people are drug seekers. There were also stories about misdiagnoses of late-stage cancer.

# SORRY AND GLAD

*for Irene*

I'm sorry that whatever happened to you happened.

I'm sorry you could never talk about it, leaving my compassion for you weak and spindly, starved of your truth.

I'm sorry you could somehow not manage to be as kind and helpful to Rob and me as you were to random strangers, to all our grandma's neighbours, to people who relied on volunteers to drive them to visit their relatives in prison, to animals.

I'm glad you were kind to all those people and animals.

I'm sorry you have lived with so much pain that you had to lock it up and guard it around the clock.

I'm sorry your pain and fear and God knows what else prevented you from being able to see Rob and me.

I'm sorry I haven't always been able to see and still sometimes can't see that you had to become as critical and harshly judgmental as you are in order to protect yourself.

I'm sorry I still need so much distance to protect myself from you.

I'm glad the distance enables us to be nicer to each other.

I'm glad you love my phone calls so much.

I'm sorry I will never be the daughter who will come to you in your old age and keep you company, help get the groceries, clean the windows, dust the high shelves, make the tea.

I'm glad you have friends who will.

I'm glad you like the mint tea I harvest from my garden and mail to you.

I'm glad so many people out there where you live see your goodness and admire and respect you.

I'm sorry I can't keep silent about how you hurt me.

I'm glad I don't agree with you about keeping silent.

I'm sorry that the small gestures you have made in my direction over the years have not made much difference to the pain I still carry from my time with you.

I'm glad you made those gestures, and I'm sorry if you don't know that.

I'm sorry what we have is not a mother-daughter relationship and sorry that the possibility of that was thoroughly extinguished long ago.

I'm glad my Elders taught me that the old ones must always be cared for and sorry you can't see that I am doing the best I can to follow that teaching by calling you once a week and twice a week when you are unwell or there is a pandemic lockdown.

I'm sorry I can't—won't ever—move out there.

I'm glad I came to understand that only hurt people hurt people.

I'm glad I wrote this.

I'm sorry that it probably won't be enough.

I'm glad that when I think of you, my heart can still ache.

we sat next to each other on the side of your bed
this was our living room during the day
our couch

the doctor had just left
we were both quietly crying
my arm draped around your bony shoulders

bereft of words
all I could say in my tear-thickened voice was
I feel like I've spent my whole life
trying to protect you

you said:

I feel like you always *have* protected me

in my darkened soul
I thought but didn't say
what the fuck can you possibly be referring to?

●-●-●

in one last glorious act
of oppositional defiance
you grew more and more luminous

it started long before your body quit
while it dwindled day by day
your spirit just got bigger
passing through the limiting border
of skin
taking up more and more space
bright and beautiful
the fragile shell that housed it
finally irrelevant

you didn't die, Rob
you shed your body
I watched you as you moved out of it
occupied the room in a different way
but that old skin, eh?
it still clings in places
even so
you shook that thing off
when it was no longer able to serve you

I watched you do it
held breathless in the mystery of
your triumph

# ONCE UPON A TIME IN A HOSPICE

Even with extra meds, Rob got to a point where he was really only comfortable in his hospital room. Everything else was a stretch. Before we gave up on the outings though, our family friend Moe and I took him to the Nic to hear my brother and his band play the Saturday matinee one last time. The Nicolette is a small hotel in St. Boniface. Its bar is the neighbourhood watering hole and the home of my mother's darts league. My brother's band, the Renegades, was the house band there for many years. Although Rob was very frail and needed to use a wheelchair, I felt confident taking him there with Moe, a nurse practitioner. Moe was given responsibility for the breakthrough narcotics we had to have on hand.

My Métis family had taken Rob in as one of their own. Rob would often go to the Nic to hear my brother's band while I was back in Nova Scotia. He also visited my birth mother, who lived conveniently across the street from "our family bar." Sometimes, they went over together to see the band. When she died three and a half years after Rob and the family gathered in Winnipeg, I slept in her room. She had taped Rob's obituary in the *Winnipeg Free Press* to her wall with Scotch tape that had dried and was starting to come off the faded and yellowed newspaper clipping.

On that cold winter afternoon, we wheeled Rob into the dark bar, our eyes adjusting from the brightness of the sunshine outside. He was bundled up with his gaunt, angular face and dark, sunken eyes looking out from under the fur Cossack hat we had borrowed from Uncle Derry. We hadn't yet reached our table when we heard my brother, the bass player, stop singing in the middle of a song and announce from the stage, while the band kept playing: "Rob Currie is in the house! Give it up for Rob Currie!" All twenty or so Saturday afternoon bar patrons clapped and cheered. Rob grinned.

Uncle Derry, not someone who frequented bars, met us there. He was always up for new experiences. Intent on checking out the gambling machines, off he went while Rob, Moe, and I settled in at our table and ordered drinks. We sent a beer over to Uncle Derry, who was sitting in front of the garishly flashing screen as if hypnotized. I don't think he had any luck there, but he did win the meat draw, another first for him.

I had been initiated into the fun if somewhat peculiar practice of the weekly meat draw during the many Saturday afternoons I spent at the Nic with my family. Bar staff sell raffle tickets throughout the afternoon, and when the band is on their last break, someone draws the tickets of the lucky winners, who receive a couple of pounds of hamburger or maybe a steak. I think Uncle Derry won a pound of bacon and a dozen eggs that day. His excitement was palpable; unbridled enthusiasm is something he has always had in great measure. When his ticket number was called, he leapt off the high stool he'd been occupying in front of the gambling machine and bounded up to the stage to collect his prize.

Rob lasted about an hour before he needed to go back to the hospital. We crammed a lot of fun into a short time.

The last drive I took with Rob was in the back of an ambulance as he was being transferred to the Grace Hospice on the grounds of Grace Hospital in St. James, just across Portage Avenue from Oakdean Boulevard, the street we had lived on when Rob first came to join our family.

On the way there, raised up a bit on his stretcher, Rob could see out the rear-door windows as the ambulance drove west on Portage. He began to comment on landmarks. I heard about friends who had lived on a particular street, his favourite dishes at Rae & Jerry's Steakhouse, and memories of Currie family Easter brunches at the Viscount Gort Hotel. As these places flashed by us on either side, I realized that he was saying goodbye to them. We passed Strathmillan Road, the other street we had lived on with our adoptive family. We had driven back in time. Soon we reached Woodhaven and the hospice.

The Grace Hospice is lovely. Airy and bright, with homey shared spaces and wide carpeted hallways leading to patients' rooms, each of which is large, with a sitting area outfitted with a table and chairs as well as a hospital bed. There were built-in drawers and shelves, one of them holding a TV. By far the best feature was the wall with large windows overlooking the snowy hills we had tobogganed down as kids. Those very same hills, outside his window.

The atmosphere was both peaceful and vibrant, not at all like a hospital—except for a few things, like the bed and the uniformed nurses coming into the rooms to go about their practice of comfort care.

Rob loved it there. He breathed easier, slept better. His sense of humour rebounded.

One night, Uncle Derry, Aunt Charlene, Moe, and I were there, our chairs in a loose semicircle around Rob in his bed, all of us looking out the windows into the blue dusk of winter. Rob would zone in and out, dozing or not, depending on when his last infusion of opiates had been. The rest of us were enjoying glasses of wine. Alcohol was permitted, as the patients were encouraged to make the place their home. The conversation led to some off-colour remark by Aunt Charlene that cracked us all up.

"It's too bad Rob missed that," I said, laughing.

Just then, Rob's eyes popped open, and he feigned a shocked look. He hadn't missed a thing. He was resting comfortably on the web of love we wove around him.

When the four of us had polished off the first bottle of wine, I offered to get a second bottle from my car that I'd intended to bring to a friend's place for supper the next day. It was the weekend; there was a bit of a raucous atmosphere developing in Rob's room. I put on my coat and headed out to the car, enveloped in the velvety darkness of the Manitoba winter night.

I grabbed the wine and headed back inside—but when I got to the front door, it was locked. I had forgotten: after nine, you had to press a buzzer for a staff person to let you in. I pressed the buzzer and instantly regressed to my deviant teenage self, hiding the bottle under my coat, holding it in place with my arm, nonchalantly, I hoped. I wasn't breaking any rules, and I was well over the legal drinking age, but I also didn't feel like broadcasting our little soiree to the nursing staff. As the nurse approached the glass door, I smiled at her as if there were nothing strange about the bottle-shaped bulge on my left side. She let me in, and as I stepped inside, the bottle clinked on something. I tried not to look guilty. I was giddy with stress and exhaustion and the defiant happiness we were basking in that evening. I made it back to the room without incident. There was a general expression of glee from everyone when I produced the bottle with a bit of a flourish. Mission accomplished.

We carried on well into the night, filling Rob's room with happiness and hijinks.

# Interlude

You are the pulled tooth, rotten, that made me ill, had to go. Now my tongue keeps going to that empty, tender place, savouring the soreness there in a fucked-up way.

The ways we are both colonized clash like rutting bull moose locking horns. You strike: I am not a real NDN because I don't want to be with someone who gets high every night and am not much for gambling. Because I have no appetite for juicy gossip about other people's dramas, don't feel the need to get all the latest dirt. Because I don't believe my not wanting to be with you justifies all the myriad acts of meanness you enact upon the corpse of our love.

I am the one being challenged. I try to stand my ground, the sacred ground of my homeland, where my ancestors' bones grow what makes me strong. The land I still carry inside me even though I ran away from it to escape the white people there who were always trying to rip me from myself. Just like when I'm with them, with you, I can't be who I am. You can't see me; my wounded spirit twists me up differently than yours twists you up, my deformities are different from yours.

I see the colonizer in you, trying to make me white so when you look at me, you can see yourself reflected back as the real NDN in this relationship, the way some men make women feel small so they can see themselves as bigger than they actually are.

When I look at you now, I see the colonizer dressed up as an L'nu lover, one who can't let go of me, not even when all that's left is the satisfaction you get from knowing you can still hurt me. You want to be with me in spite of yourself in a way that is spiteful of yourself, you are beside yourself, outside yourself, looking for something missing inside yourself, but I don't have it.

You don't want to connect with me. You can't even fucking see me. You want to wrestle in the mud and call it foreplay, but I don't find that sexy, not with you. You just want to win. I just want to breathe.

V

# DRUM BEATS

I

*Kepmite'tmnej ta'n teli l'nuwulti'kw*
*Ni'kma'jtut mawita'nej*

shaky voices
uncertainty creating unintended syncopation
words floating loosely on the melody
every woman here has heard this Honour Song
many times
it's in our hearts
our heads
our spirits
it sounds perfect there

this is the first time we have sung it out loud
searching each other's faces for clues
direction
remembrance of how it goes
encouragement
we keep singing
all four rounds

because our Elder asked us to
Magit held our circle steady
grounded and guided us
we shared stories that night
about our ancestors
how they give us strength
and hope

when everyone had spoken
she said

we should sing the Honour Song
we knew she was right

so we stood up
wavering voices
a little bit stronger each round

it

felt

so

good

as the last note faded
we stood a moment in
sacred silence

then
turned to each other
exclaiming
amazed
hey!
next time we have a special occasion here
we won't need to ask Sylvia from the
neighbouring reserve to
come and sing the Honour Song

we can do it
ourselves

*Let us greatly respect our being L'nu*
*My people, let us gather*

II

before I found my people
I found drumming


congas
djembes
shakers
tamborims
surdos
tablas


took classes
every percussion workshop I could find


Afro-Cuban
African
South Indian
Brazilian
I drummed my way around the world
on my way home
to a circle of women drumming
me standing next to my sister
the Elder in the western direction
who had just led the third round
pointing to me with her chin
no discussion
I'm standing in the north
I'm leading the fourth and
I do it
My sister's drum beating beside me
holding me steady

III

I wanted drumming at my baby's birth to
honour their arrival and
for another reason that
I didn't know about until after

my friend had agreed to come with her hand drum
joining the baby's dad
my labour coach and my friend who was taking pictures

we brought sweetgrass into the delivery room
smudged quickly before the nurses could say
we weren't allowed

I had some complications from a maverick placenta that
separated itself from me before the birth
alerted by the bleeding, I had come to the hospital
was told I had to be induced
the bleeding stopped just in time
our birthing plan could go ahead
with the addition of a fetal heart monitor
if anything went awry we would cut to the chase
cut the child out of me

I called my drummer friend and told her
it might not go the way we hoped
or it might but
it's an hour's drive to the hospital
you could stay home and drum for us there
we would still be held close in that heartbeat

she came
her drumming ebbed and flowed through the hours of labour
an ancient tidal rhythm I floated on

we turned the volume down on the heart monitor
choosing not to be hypervigilant
we could see the red digital numbers if we looked at the machine
telling us the number of heartbeats per minute
mostly
we let the nurse attend to it
one time I looked over
saw the numbers going up
my baby's heart was starting to race

should we be concerned about that, I asked
knowing the main concern was if the heart rate dropped
we'll keep an eye on it, the nurse replied calmly

my friend came to the bedside with her drum
turned the volume up enough so we could hear
tiny, rapid little beats, then
she began to drum
matching her drumming to my baby's beating heart
gradually
in almost imperceptible increments

slowing

her drumming

down

the baby's heart

matching her

beat

for beat

# IV

whether it's glancing over at Magit
who lost her language in residential school
standing onstage two drummers over
singing her heart out in Mi'kmaw
head tilted upward
eyes closed so
happy and at peace in that moment

whether it's Lena hitting her rattle so hard against the palm of her
wrinkled hand
it literally flies off the handle and rolls noisily across the stage
in the middle of a song
Elders giggling and snorting as they try to keep singing
me only able to hold it together by not looking at them
all of us waiting until after the performance to
double over and almost piss ourselves
laughing

whether it's going to the North End Women's Drum group practice in
Winnipeg with
my oldest sister or
circling up with the Strong Water Women in Niagara with
my other sister or
picking up my We'koqma'qewiskwa drumming sisters in Unama'ki
on the way to practice
stopping at Tim's for coffee and tea for everyone
on the way to the hall

whether it's drumming for the grandmothers from sub-Saharan Africa at
a conference in Toronto held by the Stephen Lewis Foundation, then
lending them our drums so they could share
their traditional songs and dances with us
smiles and hugs transcending the language barrier

whether it's drumming on so many marches and protests
for our missing and murdered sisters
for our moderate-livelihood fishers
for our Two-Spirited and trans and Indigiqueer relatives
for the land and lakes and rivers
threatened with destruction by that bully
colonial capitalism

whether it's my child's response to the drum
when they were still inside me or
the countless little ones who crowd around
after any drumming event in our community
just wanting to hold the drum
just wanting to hit it
then toddling happily away with it
an indulgent drummer trailing a little way behind
giving the child space with this feeling

whether it's Malglit
who joined our drum group after
coming home from living away from the community
loving the songs
loving being a part of this
even though the song we sing about the residential school
makes her cry every time
for the little one she still
carries inside her

whether it's standing at the front of the room
in the funeral parlour
beside the photo of our brother with his crooked grin and
the urn that holds what's left of his physical presence
my two sisters and two grandnieces
this broken family gluing itself together
to drum and sing him home

drumming is

my healing

# NIIZHOZIIBEAN—TWO RIVERS VII

It is important not to romanticize the rivers.

In the years before and since Elzéar Goulet's death in the Red River, many more have died. Too many Indigenous lives lost and bodies found in these rivers. A young man from a First Nation in Manitoba, a troubled teenage boy in foster care, believed to have jumped off the St. Vital Bridge in 2013. Tina Fontaine's body pulled out of the Red in 2015, wrapped in plastic and weighted to make it sink and stay on the bottom. Only two of so many, some whose names we know, some whose names are lost. Every child matters, every life matters. The belief that many of the terrifyingly high number of Missing and Murdered Indigenous Women and Girls (MMIWG) might be in its depths led to the Drag the Red initiative being organized in 2014, coordinated searches involving community volunteers who went out in boats and lowered metal bars with hooks and chains into the river, hoping to find remains.

I walk and drum and sing in the Sisters in Spirit marches every year in Mi'kma'ki, ensuring that all our lost sisters and their grieving family members are loved and remembered, while in Winnipeg, events to honour the MMIWG are often walks along the riverbanks.

A recent memory: Thanksgiving Day, 2019. We had gathered in Winnipeg to say goodbye to our brother, who had just died. The first and only time in my life so far that I was with all but one of my living siblings at the same time. We had gathered a few years earlier, when Maman died, but the one who we had just buried hadn't been able to join us. This time, thirteen people in my family, from three generations, had brunch at the Original Pancake House, located in the upscale development at the Forks. After our meal, we walked down the trail to my sister's sculpture, *Niimaamaa*, created in collaboration with two other Indigenous women artists, at the southernmost point of the

240

junction of the two rivers. The name for this spot, Niizhoziibean, had been revealed by Elders Barbara and Clarence Nepinak in a traditional Naming Ceremony held in August 2018, then officially adopted by the City of Winnipeg to honour the history of our Indigenous people.

*Niimaamaa* means "my mother" and is a word recognized by Anishinaabemowin, Cree, and Michif speakers. She is a strikingly beautiful thirty-foot sculpture made of polished and painted corten steel, wearing a copper dress to symbolize prosperity, as copper kettles have long been understood to connote wealth in our cultures. She is pregnant, a water carrier, and she kneels in humility and reverence, looking eastward to the rising sun. Seven strands of her hair cascade to the ground behind her, representing the Seven Sacred Teachings. Within the strands, the waterways of the Red and Assiniboine rivers are honoured. She is Mother Earth, honouring all forms of life as her children. Her highly polished metal skin allows everyone to see themselves reflected in her.

This was the not the first time I had been to visit *Niimaamaa*, but it was the first time I saw her with my oldest sister there, explaining her creation and its meaning in depth to us. I have priceless photos of us there that day, the young ones climbing up and down the semicircular stone wall that embraces the sculpture, my two brothers, two sisters, and me posing for pictures to document this rare moment.

There, on the banks of the rivers we live and die by, my people, my family, my truest self.

# A FEW QUESTIONS

is the ability to walk away from the ashes of
what used to be your house
and ask directions to the nearest shelter
a quality?

what are we doing when we spout
admiration for survival in the face of
cataclysmic destruction from
centuries of violence
if not cowering from the truth?

is the mad horse of grief galloping recklessly
on the banks of a river that is a mass grave
heedless of the danger of falling in
or drawn to the depths of loss
because more of the family is down there
than back at home?

when we romanticize resilience
aren't we just turning a nasty necessity
into a glowing compliment?

Trickster, we need you
only you can twirl and dance with danger
until the droplets of your sweat fly
and swirl, splintering simpering praise
making waves from our muted dreams
that we can ride to the other side of that river
where our laughter is the crackle of lightning
cleaving the weighted air
illuminating an encampment
where we gather
grinning and feasting
on all the free joy

# YOU WEIGH THE WORTH

On the one hand:

1. Being protected from overt racism as a light-skinned, white-passing Métis child schooled in the mannerisms of white people
2. Always having enough to eat, clothes to wear that were appropriate for each season, and stable housing
3. Growing up with the understanding that I had many options and opportunities
4. A private school education for part of high school
5. Growing up with the assumption that I would attend post-secondary education and gain knowledge and skills that would enable me to be financially self-sufficient
6. Access to extracurricular activities like piano and swimming lessons
7. The privilege of getting out of the city on a regular basis to spend time in nature
8. Being encouraged in my love of reading and books
9. Camping vacations and visits to farms where family friends lived

On the other hand:

1. The constant pressure to be somebody I could never be
2. Intermittent physical abuse and constant emotional abuse
3. The impossibility of growing up whole and strong
4. Equally strong feelings of longing for and fear of connection
5. Helplessly watching my little brother be systematically dismantled before my eyes
6. Damnably persistent difficulty attaching to another human being
7. An ever-present sense of wandering alone in a wilderness
8. All-pervasive loneliness
9. The meandering river of melancholy that runs through my heart
10. Always the feeling of deeply missing someone or something as yet unknown
11. Living with the knowledge that I have been a pawn in a game of what Chelsea Vowel calls "adoption as cultural annihilation,"[42] leaving me a cultural amputee
12. A lifetime of psychic surgeries to remove cancerous colonial concepts and ways of thinking, the goal being to get it all, but knowing I never will
13. Not having a mother to turn to since a small child
14. The constant, exhausting search for home

You weigh the relative worth.

◆ ● ●

*Maarsii*, Creator, for ceremony. In the lodge, all this dissolves, and I am simply who I was born to be.

# POINT MICHAUD

Rob died on August 30, 2012, a couple of months before his fifty-first birthday.

I was back home in Unama'ki—well, not home exactly. I was staying at a beach house in Point Michaud, on the eastern side of the island, with my son and the woman who was my girlfriend at the time.

●●●

The wheels of my suitcase rolled along on the shiny waxed floor of the hallway in the palliative care ward. In every room I passed, someone lay quietly dying in the sunny late-summer morning. A bag hung from my left shoulder, I gripped another one in my left hand, and my right hand pulled my carry-on suitcase as I made my way to the elevator. My taxi to the airport was already waiting outside the front entrance to the hospital. As I passed the nurses' station, the nurse on duty looked up, the judgment in her eyes searing into me: how could I be leaving when Rob was so close to death?

I was too tired to care about what she thought. I knew that I did not owe anyone an explanation. I had made so many trips to be with Rob, leaving my child with friends for weeks at a time that added up to months that added up to a very large chunk of the past year. It was the end of August, school would be starting soon, we had not done any-thing together in the way of a summer vacation, and it was his birthday the next day. Rob was hanging around the doorstep of his death, no longer conscious but not yet ready to walk through. I had promised to do everything in my power to be there when he died, but now I had to go home. I spent a quiet morning with him, telling him in my heart and out loud how much he meant to me, how much I loved him and always would, then somehow I found the strength to kiss his hollowed yet peaceful face one last time and walk out into the hallway with all my baggage.

It was so quiet. I could hear every footfall as I walked away from my dying brother. I was too exhausted to cry.

exhaustion takes our tears
they disappear
into the same place where
all the deep breaths we cannot take
lay heavy and dense
waiting for
that moment when
finally

we can

just

be

• • •

We had been coming to this beach house for a number of years. Only an hour-and-a-half's drive from home took us to the east coast of the island and a completely different environment from where we lived on the western shoreline. The beach was a three-kilometre expanse of sand, spiky grass anchoring the dunes along the border. Cranberry bogs encircled streams and lagoons where freshwater springs and surging tides met. To get to the point beyond the beach, you had to hike, which involved taking off your shoes and rolling up your pant legs to cross a stream.

It was still swimming season in late August, although the sea there, open to the North Atlantic, was much colder than the balmy temperature of the water I had grown used to where I lived. Chilly water notwithstanding, we were spending our days at Point Michaud on the beach.

My son had befriended a young British boy around his age who lived near Sherwood Forest in England and spent time every summer in Unama'ki, as his parents had bought land nearby. My Mi'kmaw girlfriend asked him what he knew about the original people whose homeland his family visited every summer. His complete ignorance led to an abridged Mi'kmaw history lesson, and when he heard about the horrific treatment of the Mi'kmaq by his ancestors, he exclaimed in his delightful accent: "Bloody bastards!" We still quote him to this day, and it never fails to make us laugh.

It was fortuitous for my son to have a friend to meet up with on the beach each day, because part of me was still in Winnipeg. The beach house had no cell service, and it would have defeated the purpose of our last-minute family vacation for me to stay by the landline all day, so every couple of hours, I came in to call Uncle Derry for an update on Rob. My brother was lingering, biding his time.

During one phone conversation, our uncle expressed his amazement at the situation: Rob had been beyond eating or drinking for days. We had no idea what was keeping him going. Uncle Derry's stamina was waning. I wavered between worrying that Rob was waiting for me to show up again and worrying that I was being egotistical. I was also worried about our uncle, who, in his late seventies, was picking up my slack. I tried talking to Rob telepathically, telling him it was okay to go. There were several phone calls with no change. We were poised on the edge of a cliff, the ground shifting under our feet.

Then I remembered a conversation Rob and I had had months earlier, one of the rare times we talked openly about how he felt about dying.

"I'm kind of looking forward to seeing Kassie again," he had said.

Kassie was his first child. She had died one day after her birth, having contracted a strep virus while passing through the birth canal. Rob's wife had been routinely swabbed in the early stages of labour, but in yet another tragedy, there had been a mix-up, and the lab results hadn't come back in time for medication to be administered to my sister-in-law that could have prevented their baby from getting sick. I never met Kassie, but I visited her grave with Rob whenever I was in Winnipeg.

I phoned Uncle Derry and told him this, the one thing I had heard Rob say that had helped take away his fear of dying. Since a dying person's ability to hear is often the last sense to go, I suggested that he comfort Rob by reminding him that Kassie was waiting for him on the other side. Then I walked the beach and prayed to the niece I'd never had the chance to meet, asking her to come and take her dad home.

I called again about an hour later. Uncle Derry's voice was peaceful as he told me that when he returned to Rob's bedside after our last conversation, he had taken Rob's bony hand in his and reminded him that Kassie was waiting for him. Rob, in the first sign of consciousness he'd shown in two days, had squeezed our uncle's hand, let go, and died.

this morning
dawn broke beautifully
orange exuberance warming the distant horizon
of the glittering Atlantic

the beach house room
more windows than walls
welcomes the first light
my lover and my son still asleep

this morning
much like any other
offers no sign that today is different; it's
my interior landscape that is marked by the change
all peace and emptiness

today I awaken to a world that
no longer has my brother in it
all is quiet except for the soothing
rhythmic rolling of the waves
just a smooth
polished stone's throw away

life and death in a watery embrace
pulling back from the shore, then releasing over
and over
wave
after wave crashing
into its own soft demise

this is the sound eternity makes

●●●

I did not go to Winnipeg for Rob's funeral. I wouldn't have been able to grieve the loss of him in the presence of our adoptive mother. Maman went, though, as did one of my brothers, whom she wheeled into the church, leaning on his wheelchair handles for support as if it were also her walker. It was the only time my two mothers met.

Rob was cremated, and Uncle Derry saw to it that some of the ashes were sent to me. I cast them into the sea in the four directions in four separate ceremonies at different places along the coastline around Unama'ki, my beautiful island home that Rob never got to see. I drummed and sang one round of the Mi'kmaw Honour Song at each place.

We started, of course, in the east, walking the beach at Point Michaud—the same place the waves had soothed me when I lost him for the second and final time. We hiked out to the headland and scattered his ashes on the cresting waves.

Some are Born to sweet delight
Some are Born to Endless Night

—WILLIAM BLAKE[43]

Me.

And Rob.

# STORIES UNTOLD

I gave my testimony at a gathering of Sixties Scoop survivors in Winnipeg in 2018. It was hosted by the Sixties Scoop Department of the Manitoba Métis Federation. There was a quiet room in the hotel set aside from the larger gathering and a tech person to do the video recording. Similar to the recordings of residential school survivors telling their stories at the Truth and Reconciliation Commission events, the purpose of this was to enter our stories into the historical record of this country, from which they had been missing.

We were allowed to have a support person with us. I was surprised and touched that five people from my two families attended: my birth family brothers who lived in Winnipeg, my sister-in-law, one of my nephews, and my uncle Derry.

It was tough, but their presence gave me strength. I read a written overview of my experiences, not trusting myself to be able to speak spontaneously in that setting, then finished by playing and singing my song "Lost Moccasin."

> A baby girl left to find her way
> The miracle of birth betrayed her
> And somewhere out there a mother prays
> She's in the hands of the Creator
> Questions coming as she grows
> Answers she may never know
> Lost Moccasin, Lost Moccasin
> I know it's hard to trust
> Lost Moccasin, Lost Moccasin
> You must

A little girl trying to find her place
Along a path she cannot follow
And every day she wears a happy face
Although inside she feels so hollow
Searching for a ray of light
How to make this come out right
Lost Moccasin, Lost Moccasin
You've got to sing your song
So Lost Moccasin, Lost Moccasin
Move on

So she followed her dreams
Right out of town
She rode the rails and the Greyhound
Believing that what goes around must surely come around
Oh, it must surely come around

Young woman now out on the road
So many places she could go
So many things that she needs to unload
So many things she wants to know
Then one day she gets a call
Magic happens after all
Lost Moccasin, Lost Moccasin
There's nowhere left to go
Lost Moccasin, Lost Moccasin
Come home

So she followed her dreams
Right back to that town
She rode the rails and the Greyhound
Knowing that what goes around surely comes around
Oh, it most surely comes around

A woman now with a baby boy
And their true home is with each other
No gift more precious, no greater joy
She gives thanks for being a mother
Answers she can give her child
How he came to be so wild
Lost Moccasin, Lost Moccasin
Coming home at last
Lost Moccasin, Lost Moccasin
Stop running so fast
Lost Moccasin, Lost Moccasin
Make peace with the past
Lost Moccasin, Lost Moccasin
Come home, come home, come home

After it was over, my uncle was the one who was most distressed. My Métis family members were glad I was speaking my truth, but the content came as no shock to them. One of my two brothers there had grown up in the child welfare system, and they had all survived their own versions of broken families, abandonment, and abuse. It was typical of the generosity of Indigenous people to offer comfort in a situation like this to the settler relative who found my story hard to hear.

My uncle expressed deep regret about what I had gone through, wondering aloud why I had not told him about these things when they were happening. I tried to explain how abuse steals the voices of children and how, when I was older, I felt I had to respect his relationship with his brother—my adoptive father—whom he dearly loved. He shook his head with an expression of both sadness and confusion; I could almost see his mind recalibrating what he thought he had known about my adoptive family. While my birth family members were feeling proud and strengthened by my courage, he was disoriented, his eyes wet with tears. We encircled him in a group hug.

That poignant moment aligned with the teachings I had received from Elders in both Métis and Mi'kmaw communities about how generosity is a core value in our cultures. Thinking about it now reminds me of a Mi'kmaw woman I had worked with for years in We'koqma'q who had a staggering array of chronic mental and physical health issues but who told me one day, when I arrived at her home for our appointment, that the family of a person in our community who had just died needed me more than she did right then, and so I should go and be with them; she was giving up her time with me that week. Generosity: How we can pivot on a dime, away from our own needs, to support someone whose needs we see as greater. This is one of many shining examples of how we live our belief in interconnectedness. How turning the attention away from ourselves is sometimes an expression of just how healthy we're still able to be, despite intense adversity. How resilient our capacity to love is.

We packed up and dispersed; I was heading home with one of my brothers to his house in the North End, where I was staying.

The two of us were silent in the musty elevator. When the heavy steel doors slid open and emptied us out onto the main floor, the two of us headed down a carpeted hallway toward the double glass doors to the parking lot, him carrying my guitar.

"Hey," I said, catching up to his long stride so I was walking beside him, "I know all that stuff I said might have stirred stuff up for you. You okay?"

He replied, "I have stories I've never told anyone."

I didn't know the details about the foster homes he had lived in—how many there were, what they were like. I just knew they hadn't kept him from ending up on the street as a teenager for some hardscrabble years of fending for himself. Somewhere along that road, he made a good friend, and when he found his way back to our mother, he brought this friend with him.

The only time I ever saw this brother's feelings surface and flow out of him in tears of grief and gratitude was when that lifelong friend who also became our brother died. I think losing him was harder for my brother than any of the rest of us will ever fully grasp. Because when he was alive, my brother did not carry all his secrets alone. I have a vague sense of this, a sketch whose outline is blurred by a watercolour wash, because that's how it was with Rob and me. The two of us didn't have to talk about it, but when he was on the planet, there was someone who kept company with the deepest part of me.

For each of us, when that person was in our lives, we were not alone. Because they knew.

# Postlude

a river people
cannot be contained
defined
detained
refined
raw as the green reeds
awash in a marshy
contradiction
land or lake
river or delta
the landscape shifts

space for mystery
multiplicity

a river people
are most at home in motion
living in the flow between
what is concealed
and what is revealed
curiosity a current
singing in our veins

a river people
tumble over stones
that sparkle in the sun
smooth soothing river song
wears down our rough edges
makes us shine

a river people
know what to leave
and what to take
when to pause
in the intervals
where the river turns
where there's a shore
not there before
or anymore
the next time

we dance between form
and the force of a river

a river people
move with the energy of a river
love with the energy of a river
rising
flowing
trickling
hurtling

deep and musical
moving water

# ACKNOWLEDGMENTS

Rob, we did this together, you know that. My spirit would not have survived without your brave and fragile one bound to it the way it always was and still is.

Rowan, the reason for my journey and my North Star. The best day of my life was the day I had the honour of bringing you into the world. Creator helped me to find my way back to myself just before you were born so you would always know who you are and be able to stand up strong and proud, carried on the shoulders of our ancestors. I see them in you, in your courage to be yourself, in how you don't hesitate to speak up about injustice, in your love for the land. I hear them in your music and your writing and see them in your art. We are all so proud of you.

My ancestors have always been with me, whether I was aware of them or not. Now that I am, I source such strength and guidance from their presence and their example. Elzéar, your fierce pride courses through my veins, and Grandma, I feel your love like a wrinkled hand on my cheek. Your intellectual curiosity and high expectations for yourself and others fuel my passions and my creativity. I am humbled and blessed to follow in the footsteps of all who went before me.

My brothers Les, Freddie, Lindsay, and Buff, for the warm strength in those first welcoming hugs and the steadfast love we rekindled that has sweetened every day since. My sisters Val, Laurie, Heather, and Gigi. I never got to meet you, Laurie and Heather, but the way you live on in the hearts and stories of all whose lives you touched makes me feel both proud of who you were and a deep sense of loss. Val and Gigi, for the times we spent and the stories and teachings you shared with me, I am grateful. All my nieces and nephews, for the joy of knowing you and the amazing ways you carry our family's beauty and strength forward! Chelsea, for your sweetness and smarts. Brandi, for your integrity and vision and for raising such lovely boys. Sam, for the passion we share for our family's history and the immense dignity of our ancestors, which I have seen bring tears to your eyes, and for adding such a stunningly beautiful family to our clan. To the aunties, uncle, and cousins who have drawn me into our family circle, what a blessing to be kin with you all. Bridget, for the special connection we share and for being the rock that you are, not just for me but for so many.

Claudette, if you hadn't been willing to meet me, I'd still be living in the half-light. *Maarsii*, Maman.

Ray, for having known that something was not right and opening up to tell me so after all these years, which was so healing.

Uncle Derry and Charlene, you are the only people who have shared my whole life with me. Thanks for showing me what unconditional love is and for asking me to be Vincent's godmother—none of us knowing at the time that he and I had the Sixties Scoop in common. I hope to live up to the trust you placed in me when I was just sixteen years old. Vince, may my healing and your healing weave their way into a strong thread in the fabric of our lives.

Friends who've become family along the way: Jennine, Jody, Adrienne, Cat, Ariella, Ann, Lyse, Elizabeth, John, De-Ann, Nancy, Katie, Charlotte, Ann, Kate, Elaine, Hannah, Gillian, Scott, Clifford. Thanks for holding me steady.

All the Sixties Scoop survivors I've met along the way: Bill, Nel, Jocelynne, David, Albert, Tanja, and all the others. Knowing you has given me strength, and the compassion you have for all the characters in our messy lives grounds me. So glad to have, or to have had (Rest in Power, Bill), your companionship on this journey.

My beloved Elders: Albert Marshall and Malglit Pelletier, you were instrumental in bringing me to We'koqma'q and helping me find my feet there. Magit Poulette, Auntie Caroline Gould, and Murdena Marshall, may you Rest in Power and take a break from your "what you got?" game in the Spirit World to hear me honour you for your generosity, your teachings, your laughter, your love and support. Jane Meader, Paulina Meader, Miigam'agan, gkisedtanamoogk, Lawrence Wells, Kerry Prosper, Neegaunibinessikwe/Begonegeezhig (also known as Barbara Cameron), Mae Louise Campbell, and all the lodgekeepers, Pipe Carriers, sacred firekeepers, sweat sisters and brothers, midwinter longhouse gathering companions, *wela'lioq, woliwon, chi miigwech* for ceremony. It's with you that I feel most at home in myself.

The We'koqma'q residential school survivors, you will always have a home in my heart. *Wela'lioq* for teaching me that telling our stories can be healing and for breaking that trail.

shalan joudry, Amanda Peters, Eileen Sanderson, and all the women in our Indigenous women writers' group, *wela'lioq, miigwech, maarsii* for teaching this baby bird how to fly. Alicia Elliott, my first reader, for tucking into that old farmhouse in Baddeck for a week with me, at the end of which I felt like a real writer. *Nia:wen* for taking time to help an unknown, for your detailed feedback, for the clarity with which you saw my story, which helped me see it clearly too, and for being the first one to speak the words "your book." Rebecca Silver Slayter, for your warm encouragement and dextrous practical advice, you are the midwife of this writing. Sarah Faber, for believing in my work enough to ask your agent to take a look at it—what a huge help that was! Katherena Vermette, I'm humbled by your openness, kindness, wisdom, and graciousness. To have you read my manuscript and offer suggestions was more than I could have hoped for. Can I call you my big sister even if I'm older than you? Rebecca Rose, Robin Metcalfe, Camille Fouillard, and Joe Pitawanakwat-Trudeau, I could not hope for better companions on this writer's path.

The Shean Poets and Writers Collective, for all the Saturday morning conversations and thoughtful feedback on earlier drafts of some of the pieces in this book, I thank you. You've made me a better writer.

My relatives in the Indigenous Circle Chapter of the Canadian Counselling and Psychotherapy Association, seeing myself reflected in your hearts, your visions, and your warrior's stamina in the work of helping our peoples heal has helped me find my way home. *Mahsi cho, kukstemc, ekosani, miigwech, maarsi, nia:wen, nakkumek, wela'lioq.*

All the women of Four the Moment, thanks for twenty-plus years of learning how to use our voices to sing truth to power and celebrate the beauty of our communities.

My Transformational Leadership Initiative community, y'all bring the joy! The bright fire we stoke and dance around when we're together and the embers we carry when we're not inspire me for days that add up to a lifetime of loving the world into transformational change.

The Writers' Federation of Nova Scotia is a treasure chest of every type of support imaginable. I'm grateful to have been the recipient of the Nova Scotia Indigenous Writer's Residency and the Rita Joe Indigenous Writers' Retreat at the lovely Jampolis Cottage in Avonport, Nova Scotia.

The Canada Council for the Arts' Creating, Knowing and Sharing Program provided funding that enabled me to produce the first draft of this book, and I am most grateful.

Samantha Haywood, for crushing it as an agent who balances easy-goingness with professionalism, empathy with practicality, sharing knowledge with being open to learn, and solid support with encouragement to take steps on my own. Thanks for being a champion of this book. Brian, Catharine, Jazmin, and everyone else at Arsenal Pulp, for "getting" my work; I knew right away that my book had found the right portal into the world. Catharine, your masterful editing brought significant and subtle improvements. Jazmin, your ability to envision and execute a book design that aligns so beautifully with the writing within seems like magic to me. Brian, you are steering a very cool ship, and I'm so happy to be on board!

# ENDNOTES

1   Darren Major and Olivia Stefanovich, "Judge Approves Historic $23B
    First Nations Child Welfare Compensation Agreement," CBC News,
    October 24, 2023, https://www.cbc.ca/news/politics/judge-approves-23
    -billion-first-nations-child-welfare-agreement-1.7006351; First Nations
    Child & Family Caring Society of Canada, "Caring Society Statement on
    the Federal Court Approval of the 23.4B Compensation Agreement," First
    Nations Child & Family Caring Society of Canada statement, October
    24, 2023, https://fncaringsociety.com/sites/default/files/2023-10/Oct%
    2024%202023%20Statement%20on%20Federal%20Court%20Compen
    sation%20Approval.pdf; First Nations Child & Family Caring Society
    of Canada, "Update on the Human Rights Case for First Nations Kids,"
    *First Nations Child & Family Caring Society Newsletter*, Fall 2023,
    https://fncaringsociety.com/sites/default/files/2023-09/Fall%202023%
    20Newsletter.pdf.

2   Raven Sinclair, "Identity Lost and Found: Lessons from the Sixties Scoop,"
    *First Peoples Child & Family Review* 3, no. 1 (2007): 65–82, https://doi
    .org/10.7202/1069527ar.

3   Jeannine Carrière, *You Should Know That I Trust You … Cultural Plan-
    ning, Aboriginal Children and Adoption* (Victoria: University of Victoria,
    School of Social Work, 2007), 40, https://icwrn.uvic.ca/wp-content
    /uploads/2013/09/cultural_planning_2007_carriere.pdf.

4   Psychotherapist Pete Walker coined the term *fawn* and added it as the
    fourth *F* in the instinctive responses to trauma. Someone using the fawn
    response will try to avoid conflict or danger, keep the peace, and ensure
    their safety at the expense of their own needs.

5   In 1755, British officials established the Indian Department. Over time,
    the Indian Department transformed and came to include management of
    the northern regions of Canada. The name of the department has changed
    from the Department of Indian Affairs and Northern Development
    (DIAND) in 1966 to the Department of Aboriginal Affairs and Northern
    Development Canada (AANDC) in 2011 to Indigenous and Northern
    Affairs Canada (INAC) in 2015. In 2017, two separate departments were

created: Crown-Indigenous Relations and Northern Affairs Canada (CIRNAC) and Indigenous Services Canada (ISC).

6   Niigaanwewidam James Sinclair and Sharon Dainard, "Sixties Scoop," *The Canadian Encyclopedia*, June 22, 2016, https://www.thecanadian encyclopedia.ca/en/article/sixties-scoop.

7   Anne Bokma, "Adoptees Seeking Redress: Canada Confronts the Sixties Scoop," *ICT*, January 2, 2017, https://ictnews.org/archive/adoptees -seeking-redress-canada-confronts-sixties-scoop.

8   Kendra Cherry, "Erikson's Stages of Development: A Closer Look at the Eight Psychosocial Stages," Verywell Mind, August 3, 2022, https://www .verywellmind.com/erik-eriksons-stages-of-psychosocial-development -2795740.

9   Katy Kandaris-Weiner, "What Is the Fawning Trauma Response?" Inner Balance Counseling, July 26, 2023, https://innerbalanceaz.com/blog /what-is-the-fawning-trauma-response.

10  Nola Turner-Jensen, "Blood Memory," LinkedIn, December 18, 2019, https://www.linkedin.com/pulse/blood-memory-nola-turner-jensen/.

11  "Exploring 'Blood Memory' | Indigenous Forum," National Bioneers Conference, October 21, 2018, https://nationalbioneersconference2018 .sched.com/event/ErZi/exploring-blood-memory-indigenous-forum.

12  *Diba Jimooyung "Telling Our Story": A Guide to the Diba Jimooyung Permanent Exhibit* (Mt. Pleasant, Michigan: Ziibiwing Center of Anishi- nabe Culture & Lifeways), quoted in Mary Annette Pember, "Blood Memory," Daily Yonder, July 16, 2010, https://dailyyonder.com/blood -memory/2010/07/16/.

13  Liam J. Haggarty, "Métis Economics: Sharing and Exchange in Northwest Saskatchewan," in *Métis in Canada: History, Identity, Law & Politics*, eds. Christopher Adams, Gregg Dahl, and Ian Peach (Edmonton: Uni- versity of Alberta Press, 2013), 205–248.

14  Turner-Jensen, "Blood Memory."

15  Turner-Jensen, "Blood Memory."

16 Darold Treffert, "Genetic Memory: How We Know Things We Never Learned," *Scientific American*, January 28, 2015, https://blogs.scientific american.com/guest-blog/genetic-memory-how-we-know-things-we -never-learned/.

17 The First Nations people originally of the Great Plains between the upper Missouri and middle Saskatchewan rivers.

18 Valerie Andrews, "Stages of Reunion," Origins Canada, accessed January 3, 2024, https://www.originscanada.org/services/adoption-reunion/stages -of-reunion/.

19 Maggie Siggins, *Riel: A Life of Revolution* (Toronto: HarperCollins, 1994).

20 J.R. Léveillé, *Anthologie de la Poésie Franco-Manitobaine* (Saint-Boniface, Manitoba: Les Éditions du Blé, 1990).

21 Andrews, "Stages of Reunion."

22 *Oxford Languages*, s.v. "primal," accessed December 26, 2023, https://www .google.com/search?q=definition+of+primal&oq=definition+of+primal.

23 Manitoba Sustainable Development, Parks and Protected Spaces Branch, *Red River: A Canadian Heritage River Ten-Year Monitoring Report: 2007–2017* (Winnipeg: The Canadian Heritage Rivers Board, 2018), https://chrs.ca/sites/default/files/2020-03/Red_River_2007_to_2017 _Ten_Year_Monitoring_Report_w-french_0.pdf.

24 *Kitpu* is the Mi'kmaw word for "eagle."

25 *Ai-ai* is the Mi'kmaw word for "yes."

26 United Nations Permanent Forum on Indigenous Issues, "Indigenous Peoples, Indigenous Voices," United Nations, accessed December 27, 2023, https://www.un.org/esa/socdev/unpfii/documents/5session_factsheet 1.pdf.

27 Niigaan Sinclair, "Indigenous Identity More Than DNA," *Winnipeg Free Press*, October 19, 2018, https://www.winnipegfreepress.com/breaking news/2018/10/19/indigenous-identity-more-than-dna.

28 Sinclair, "Indigenous Identity More Than DNA."

29 Sounds of Blackness, "Livin' the Blues," YouTube video, 4:13, https://www.youtube.com/watch?v=tv5zGOwoOuo.

30 *Dit* is the French word for "known as."

31 *Dit* names were nicknames used to help tell apart different families with the same surname. These could be based on a person's personality or physical traits, their occupation, where they lived, or where they were from.

32 APA *Dictionary of Psychology*, s.v. "cultural blindness," accessed January 3, 2024, https://dictionary.apa.org/cultural-blindness.

33 Rita Joe, "I Lost My Talk," in *Song of Eskasoni: More Poems of Rita Joe* (Charlottetown: Women's Press, 1989).

34 John Soosaar, "Bernard's Lawsuit Helped Natives Worldwide," Canada.com, December 30, 2007, https://archives.algomau.ca/main/sites/default/files/2010-061_014_013.pdf.

35 Joan Weeks, "Waycobah First Nation Residential School Survivors Make Regalia for Youth as Part of Healing Process," CBC News, July 2, 2018, https://www.cbc.ca/news/indigenous/waycobah-first-nation-residential-school-survivors-make-regalia-for-youth-as-part-of-healing-process-1.4725634.

36 Joan Weeks (host), "Healing One Stitch at a Time," in *Atlantic Voice* (radio program), aired September 30, 2018.

37 DeeDee Austin, "Buried Truth," YouTube video, 3:55, https://www.youtube.com/watch?v=1xx-xHeTuQM.

38 Judith Viorst, *Necessary Losses: The Loves, Illusions, Dependencies, and Impossible Expectations That All of Us Have to Give Up in Order to Grow* (New York: Simon & Schuster, [1986] 2002), 22.

39 *Smoke Signals*, directed by Chris Eyre (1998; Los Angeles: eOne Films, 2000), DVD.

40  Ariana Kakhevicius, "Nadya Kwandibens Photographs the First Nations Experience Across Canada," *Canadian Geographic*, June 18, 2014, https:// canadiangeographic.ca/articles/nadya-kwandibens-photographs-the -first-nations-experience-across-canada/.

41  Lloy Wylie and Stephanie McConkey, "Insiders' Insight: Discrimination Against Indigenous Peoples Through the Eyes of Health Care Professionals," *Journal of Racial and Ethnic Health Disparities* 6, no. 1 (2019): 37–45, https://doi.org/10.1007/s40615-018-0495-9.

42  Chelsea Vowel, "Adoption as Cultural Annihilation," ICT, May 5, 2012, https://ictnews.org/archive/adoption-as-cultural-annihilation.

43  William Blake, "Auguries of Innocence," Poetry.com, accessed February 15, 2024, https://www.poetry.com/poem/39090/auguries-of-innocence.

**ANDREA CURRIE**, Green Turtle Woman, is a mother, writer, psychotherapist, and musician who believes that stories are medicine and that healing—of our relationships with ourselves, each other, with all creatures, and with the lands and waters of the ecosystems we're part of—has never been more important than it is now. She weaves words into pathways to personal and collective self-discovery, balancing a critique of colonial systems that continue to oppress us with the generative energy of co-creating communities where the teachings of our Elders and ancestors are honoured by living their wisdom every day, in the best way we know how.

Andrea's work in Indigenous mental health and community wellness, with all its challenges and joys, is second only to motherhood in being an immeasurable gift in her life. She experiences the core Indigenous value of reciprocity in helping with healing and being healed, in relationship and in community. Andrea lives in a constant state of gratitude for the Elders and Knowledge Keepers whose love and generosity give her the grounding and support she needs as she walks the path Creator put her on.